CW00735271

John Bendall

KENDALL'S LONGITUDE

Limited Special Edition. No. 5 of 25 Paperbacks

John Bendall

KENDALL'S LONGITUDE

AUSTIN MACAULEY PUBLISHERS™

LONDON • CAMBRIDGE • NEW YORK • SHARJAH

A CIP catalogue record for this title is available from the British Library.

ISBN 9781788239417 (Paperback)
ISBN 9781528920759 (Hardback)
ISBN 9781788239424 (Kindle e-Book)
ISBN 9781528953962 (ePub e-Book)

www.austinmacauley.com

First Published (2019)
Austin Macauley Publishers Ltd
25 Canada Square
Canary Wharf
London
E14 5LQ

To my wonderful wife, family and friends.

KENDALL'S LONGITUDE

The Times and Voyages of K2 – The Bounty Watch

'The sea life of K2…encompasses some of the most famous voyages in the annals of the oceans'

Dava Sobel, *Longitude*, 1995, p 154.

Referring to K1, K2 and K3 '…their performance was remarkable and set a standard for subsequent makers to aim for'.

Peter Poland, *The Travels of the Timekeepers*, 1991, p 18.
President of Woollahra History and Heritage Society,
2017

'This work is perhaps long overdue and will be a welcome addition to many a library'.

Rory McEvoy, Curator of Horology,
Royal Observatory, Greenwich, 2017.

THE PEOPLE, PLACES AND POLITICS

Table of Contents

Preface

Between 1770 and 1774, a London watchmaker called Larcum Kendall, working at the behest of the Board of Longitude, made a series of three 'marine timekeepers' in the form of large watches, now known as K1 (K for Kendall), K2 and K3.

Kendall's craftsmanship was superb, but his watch designs themselves brought little innovation to the technology; K1 is a copy of H4, John Harrison's famous 4th marine timekeeper. K2 and K3 are simplified designs, quicker and cheaper to manufacture.

What makes Kendall's watches intriguing is their career history. They travelled from the Arctic Circle to the South Pacific taking in North America, Australia and Africa on the way. K1 sailed with Captain James Cook to the Pacific and then with Arthur Phillip in the First Fleet to Botany Bay. K3 also sailed with Cook and later, George Vancouver.

Most remarkable in its travels was K2, Kendall's 2nd marine watch. It went to the Arctic with a young Horatio Nelson, on a voyage which nearly led to the two ships being crushed by Arctic ice. This close escape was followed by two voyages to North America, at the beginning and end of the American Revolutionary War. The British warship *Asia,* with K2 on board, landed troops to support Major Pitcairn's attack on Lexington in 1775. It was also the initial target of the first submarine attack in history. The next commission towards the end of this American war was under Rear Admiral Digby with royalty on board, and the venture was equally dangerous.

After all these adventures and an exploratory voyage to the slave coasts of West Africa, the K2-timekeeper was issued to the *Bounty* under Lieutenant William Bligh bound for Tahiti on a fateful voyage that resulted in the legendary naval mutiny. There was trouble ahead.

This is the story of K2, the *Bounty* Watch, and the adventures of many of the people whose lives it touched. As Dava Sobel wrote in her acclaimed book Longitude:

"The sea life of K2...encompasses some of the most famous voyages in the annals of the oceans."[1]

The *Bounty* Watch remained on Pitcairn's Island for over 18 years until it was rediscovered by an American sealer captain from Nantucket, which as Dava Sobel added:

"It launched K2 on yet another round of adventures."[2]

Being a power in the South Pacific, a Spanish governor decided to flex his muscles by holding the American sealer in Chile and 'confiscating' K2. This is truly a three-nation story. It took the help of a friend of Charles Darwin in the Andes and an Opium War with China, before K2 came back to Britain. There were many more moons before K2 joined the Kendall timekeepers K1 and K3, where they can now be seen at the National Maritime Museum, Greenwich.

This book focuses on the people, places and politics around K2, which witnessed so many adventures on its worldwide journeys in the hands of three maritime nations. It also tells how the three Kendall timepieces played a valuable part in finding longitude at sea in the story of time.

---

[1] Dava Sobel, *Longitude*, 1995, p154
[2] Ibid

Foreword
By Rory McEvoy

Today's visitors to the National Maritime Museum can enjoy seeing all three of Larcum Kendall's marine timekeepers in our galleries. The first and the third of this series stayed within the Admiralty's hands until recent times, when the Museum formally acquired them. The second, however, was famously lost to the Mutineers aboard the Bounty and its survival and repatriation is nothing short of a miracle. It is a distinct pleasure to be invited to write a foreword for John's book, which charts the extraordinary journey of Kendall's watch, known as K2. This work is perhaps long overdue and will be a welcome addition to many a library.

2014 saw the tercentenary of the Queen Anne Longitude Act, and the Museum marked the anniversary with a touring exhibition, entitled Ships, Clocks & Stars, which looked at the history of the Board of Longitude and the associated endeavours to enable mariners to place their longitude while at sea. Within the exhibition, Kendall's timekeepers toured the east coast of the United States, before debarking for Sydney, Australia. In total, the show was enjoyed by almost a quarter of a million visitors during its three-year duration, and the timekeepers added an estimated 25,000 miles to their travel history. At the time of writing, all three of Kendall's watches are in the Museum's horological conservation studio for condition assessment and treatment following their return from the exhibition and ahead of display in the forthcoming Pacific and Exploration galleries at the National Maritime Museum.

K2, the subject of this volume, is a substantial watch, 124mm wide; in an impressive silver case with a protective outer shell, known as a pair case, which is hallmarked for London 1771-72 by maker 'P.M.' Peter Mounier of Frith Street, Soho. The watch has what is known as a regulator-type dial, so-called as it resembles those found on the accurate pendulum clocks used by astronomers. The most significant hand marks the passage of minutes, making a full rotation in one hour; the two subsidiary dials indicate hours and seconds. The advantage of this layout is two-fold: the user can get an accurate reading of the time at a glance; and the placing of the dials in this manner simplifies the gearing behind the dial, which reduces friction and therefore helps the watch to run reliably.

The Board of Longitude commissioned Larcum Kendall to make his first watch at the cost of £450, paying him an additional £50 for the months he spent adjusting and perfecting its timekeeping. This watch, known as K1, was famously used by Captain James Cook on his second voyage of discovery (1772-5). Despite Kendall's doubts as to the durability of the design, the watch performed so well that Cook referred to it as his 'never failing guide' and in so doing, put the rubber stamp of approval on the timekeeper method of determining longitude at sea. Here was indisputable proof that the success of Harrison's watch on the two voyages to the West Indies had not been down to chance.

At £500, this design was too expensive, and so the next challenge was to produce watches that could perform just as well but at a lesser cost. Kendall agreed to make a second timekeeper for the Board of Longitude for £200. This timekeeper closely followed Harrison's design but omitted the complex rewind mechanism. Kendall's artistry as a watchmaker was second to none, but he was not an innovator. His subsequent watches did not live up to the high standards of H4/K1 and are famed instead for their life stories.

When Captain Thomas Herbert presented K2 to the Royal United Services Institute in 1843, he had the inner case engraved "This Timekeeper belonged to Captain Cook R.N..." Herbert was wrong – that honour belonged to Kendall's first longitude watch, K1. In fact, the lengthy history inscribed on the silver case is decidedly unreliable.

This book will hopefully set the record straight and add clarity to the extraordinary history of this significant navigational watch that goes beyond the mutiny of the Bounty.

Rory McEvoy,
Curator of Horology, Royal Observatory, Greenwich. 2017

PART ONE
K2 Before Pitcairn

Chapter 1
Pitcairn's Island – Lost at Sea, 1767

On 2 July, 1767, Lieutenant Philip Carteret commanding the sloop *Swallow,* sighted an island in the South Pacific Ocean. "Upon approaching it the next day, it appeared like a great rock sticking out of the sea. It was not more than five miles in circumference and seemed to be uninhabited. It was, however, covered with trees and we saw a small stream of fresh water running down one side of it. I would have landed upon it, but the surf, which at this season broke upon it with great violence, rendered it impossible."[3]

Carteret had not seen land for six days and needed more water, so sportingly offered a bottle of brandy to the first person to see land. At last, an island was sighted: "It was so high that we saw at the distance of fifteen leagues; and it being discovered by a young gentleman Robert Pitcairn who was son of Major John Pitcairn of the Royal Marines, is why we called it Pitcairn's Island."

---

[3] Carteret's Voyages, Hawkesworth 1st edition, 1773

Pitcairn Island "Rendered Impossible to Land"

Carteret logged the position of this island as 'latitude 25° 2' south, longitude 133° 21' west and about a thousand leagues to the westward of the continent of America'. Unfortunately, his longitude was wrong by nearly 200 miles which would be repeated on future naval charts. Most mariners subsequently looking for Pitcairn would not easily find it. As will be seen, this error would be a blessing to the mutineers from the *Bounty* who are part of the story of Kendall's marine timekeeper or 'sea clock' K2.

Lieutenant Philip Carteret RN was an experienced seaman who had already circumnavigated the globe. He plays an important part in this historic longitude saga, but arguably for the wrong reasons. Thanks to his reliance on outdated methods of navigation, most of the locations he reported for his discoveries – were inaccurate.

While he probably thought he was the first European to discover Pitcairn, the island was, in effect, still lost at sea.

Carteret's previous circumnavigation was under Captain John Byron (known as 'Foul-Weather Jack') who was the grandfather of the poet. Following Carteret's return from

Byron's voyage in 1766, he was invited to be captain of the *Swallow* on this exciting global voyage of discovery, accompanying the frigate *Dolphin* under the overall command of Captain Samuel Wallis.

When they sailed in 1767, Carteret was dismayed by the condition of the *Swallow* compared to Wallis's larger ship. The *Swallow* had difficulty keeping up and they got separated after passing through the Straits of Magellan.

The Dolphin and The Swallow

Carteret was suspicious that he had been abandoned by the leading ship while Wallis later blamed the weather. Fortunately, Wallis had the foresight to give Carteret sealed orders – to go on alone, in the event of separating.[4]

Sailing with Byron in April 1765, Carteret had visited the Juan Fernandez Islands in the Pacific to boost the crew's health. Scurvy had set in and the crew needed rest, fresh vegetables and meat, which the islands could provide. Goats and seals were plentiful but Byron identified another threat; "the sea abounded with sharks of an enormous size, which, when they see a man in the water, would dart into the very surf to seize him. One of them upward of 20 feet long came close to one of our boats and having seized a large seal, instantly devoured it as a mouthful."[5]

---

[4] HG Mowat, Carteret & Voyage of the Swallow
[5] Carteret's Voyages, Hawkesworth 1st edition, 1773

Once Carteret had cleared the Straits of Magellan, he repeated his earlier voyage by heading straight for the Juan Fernandez archipelago. They stayed on the islands of Mas Afuera until the crew were cleared of scurvy. It was noticeable that crews generally suffered more from scurvy than officers and gentlemen. These islands would, coincidentally, also play a part eighteen years later in the story of the K2 watch as the scene of Spanish government piracy.

Carteret then sailed west and on 2 July 1767 had his historic chance encounter with Pitcairn's Island. After logging Pitcairn, he continued his voyage by heading in a north-westerly direction to pick up favourable winds and to discover more territory for Britain. He was anxious to find islands where he could easily land, since they always needed more fresh water and food to ward off scurvy. To make matters worse, the *Swallow* was springing leaks.

On 12 August 1767, he came across a group of islands which he named Queen Charlotte's Islands. They actually appeared to have been the Solomon Islands, which the Spanish had already discovered in 1568. There was time for some repairs, but a party ashore under the ship's master, Mr Simpson, started chopping down a palm tree for fresh coconuts, which was a diplomatic disaster.

The Polynesians were initially friendly but began remonstrating with the visitors and events escalated, leading to shots and hand-to-hand fighting. Seven of the *Swallow's* crew were injured, partly by arrows fired from bows the size of medieval longbows.[6] Four sailors, including the thoughtless Mr Simpson, died of their injuries and were committed to the deep. Carteret was furious about this completely unnecessary incident and sulked for days.

By the end of August 1767, Carteret reached New Britain and discovered it was two islands instead of the one, as believed by the 17th-century explorer Dampier. After a week's rest, the journey continued and Carteret added to his list of islands: New Hanover, Portland and on 15 September, Admiralty Island.

---

[6] The Polynesian Bow was 6' 6" long with flat back and convex front. 48 lbs draw could send a 5' arrow 160 yards but erratic over long distances without flight feathers

The southern end of the Philippines was home to hostile inhabitants so they sailed to Macassar in the Dutch East Indies only to find the Dutch equally hostile. Eventually, he reached Batavia, which after major repairs, he left in September 1768, rounding the Cape of Good Hope in December and arriving back in England in March 1769.

Most of Carteret's chart locations were wrong because the problem of determining longitude at sea had not yet been cracked. Adding to the difficulties for navigators, some positions were deliberately changed on maps to deceive competitors.

Who really first discovered Pitcairn? American historian Walter Hayes states "that it was still shown on some charts as Encarnacion de Quiros, after the sixteenth century Portuguese navigator Pedro Fernandez de Quiros, who had chosen a prettier and more evocative name which exemplifies his own reaction: Sagittaria"[7]. This is still debatable, but if the island was Pitcairn, the date recorded was 13 February 1606.[8]

Quiros was Portuguese, but he sailed under the Spanish flag in a Spanish ship and was largely funded by Spanish and Papal purses. If he really did find Pitcairn, it must surely be defined as a Spanish discovery. His permission, support and finance were dependent on all claims being "on behalf of Spain"[9]. He had sailed from Callao on 21December 1605 with two modest ships and a small launch, entering the Pacific from east to west via the Straits of Magellan.

The obvious candidates for first discovery are the Polynesians. The native Tahitians accompanying the *Bounty* mutineers in 1790 quickly confirmed that Pitcairn had been inhabited by their own people. Subsequent studies indicate their previous residency went back hundreds of years.

One glance at a map of the Pacific Ocean highlights the minuscule land mass of the scattered islands, inhabited primarily by Micronesians, Melanesians and Polynesians. According to author David Lewis, it was the Polynesians who journeyed the

---

[7] Captain from Nantucket, p134

[8] Sir John Barrow, The Mutiny, p22

[9] Voyages of Pedro Fernandez de Quiros, 1595–1606, Vol 1 intro

widest and visited or occupied the vast majority of those "remote specks of land"[10].

Western explorers were generally really impressed with both the outriggers and double canoes of the Polynesians and their navigational skills. These skills appear to have been passed down through generations by memory and experience. Apart from the sun, stars and moon, the native navigators used a wide range of other clues including wind, currents, ocean drift, types of wave, clouds and even birds.

Captain Cook on his 1st voyage was particularly interested and recorded that "these people...sail from island to island for several hundred Leagues; the sun serving them for a compass by day and the Moon and Stars by night". In late 1769, Cook was given an amazing present from Tupaia, a dispossessed chief, priest and navigator who accompanied him. It was a map of the Pacific, which it is believed Tupaia drew showing every major group of islands over 3000 miles from Fiji to the Marquesas, except for Hawaii and New Zealand.

Cook was probably the first westerner who was able to evaluate directly over time, the knowledge and wisdom of an experienced Polynesian navigator, since Tupaia accompanied him for part of his 1st voyage on the *Endeavour* until he died of fever. Tupaia had amazed the whole crew by helping Cook find new islands and being able to point to the location of Tahiti at any time of the day or night, in any weather.[11]

The second discoverers of Pitcairn were probably the Portuguese/Spanish who had their 17th-century maps and records although this is still debated. Carteret and young Robert Pitcairn in *Swallow* were probably third, but they did not land. The British *Bounty* mutineers had read Carteret's reports and by then, armed with the K2-timekeeper, were actually seeking Pitcairn. They became the first westerners to set foot on and inhabit this high, rocky Pacific island, which is today a focus of international claims for fish and minerals.

Who were midshipman Pitcairn and his military father? Young Robert was the fifteen year old gentleman who spotted it in 1767 and won a bottle of brandy for his sharp eyes. He must

---

[10] David Lewis, We the Navigators, p8

[11] Ibid, p11

have been thrilled and honoured by having an island named after him and his family.

Having joined the Royal Navy as a teenage midshipman, Robert Pitcairn was appointed to the *Swallow* in July 1766. Two years after that, he was less lucky by joining the *Aurora* which sailed in December 1769 for India. The *Aurora* was never seen again, lost with all hands en route.

Robert's father was Major John Pitcairn, who was commissioned as a lieutenant in a Marine regiment where commissions could not be purchased. He served in Canada in the Seven Years' War and will later make his mark in this 'story of time'.

After Carteret left Pitcairn in July 1767, there were three known attempts over the next forty years to find the island again. These were by Captain Cook, the mutineers in the *Bounty* and an American Quaker captain from Nantucket. These mariners all seemed to have the same map, with the same wrong longitude.

Cook gave up. "Being in the Latitude of Pitcairn's Island discovered by Captain Carteret in 1767, we looked out for it but could see nothing except two Tropical birds."[12] This was mid-1773 in the *Resolution* which returned to England in July 1775. Had Cook found Pitcairn, he would have informed the Admiralty of Carteret's error and provided an accurate position some eleven years before the *Bounty* mutineers landed. It would have changed history.

The mutineers did find Pitcairn in January 1790, over twenty years after Carteret, but it took months and with much difficulty. The inaccuracy of Carteret's charts would be a real blessing in helping them disappear and is part of the story of Kendall's marine timekeeper K2.

The captain from Nantucket did best, with modest difficulty, but he also had some information from Spanish charts.

They could all be forgiven for thinking that Pitcairn's Island really was lost at sea.

---

[12] Journal of Resolution, 2 August 1773

Discovering Pitcairn 1767 Commemorative Stamp

Chapter 2
The Nautical Problem
By Mike Dryland

When Captain Carteret and Midshipman Pitcairn logged the eponymous island on 2 July 1767, they had only a very rough idea of their position. At that time, most mariners on the ocean, when out of sight of land, had no scientific or accurate way to work out exactly where they were.

To know your precise position on the ocean, if you cannot see any established landmarks, you need ways to find 'latitude' and 'longitude'. Latitude tells you how far north or south of the equator you are; longitude tells you how far east or west you need to go.

Carteret knew his latitude pretty well. Mariners had been able to find latitude for centuries. At noon, using a quadrant (or later a sextant) to measure the angle from the horizon up to the Sun, adjusted for the date, will tell you latitude. Carteret was pretty close: he charted Pitcairn at latitude 25° 2' S (the modern position is 25° 7' S – a latitude error of only about 9 km).

But Carteret was guessing at his longitude, most probably calculated by 'dead reckoning' – a guesstimate based on speed and course since his last position. He charted Pitcairn at longitude 133° 21' W: the modern position is 130° 11' W – Carteret was over 3 degrees of longitude in error (around 300 km). This was to have consequences.

Finding longitude is not easy. You need to know the time, accurately, in two places at the same moment. Specifically, you need to know the time difference between local time at your position and the time at home, Greenwich say, at the same instant. Every 4 minutes' difference is the same as 1 degree of longitude – an hour's difference is the same as 15 degrees. This is because the Sun appears to go once around the Earth, 360 degrees, in a day of 24 hours. In one hour, the Sun moves overhead by 360 divided by 24 = 15 degrees.

Local time you can get from the Sun – it crosses your own 'meridian' (the imaginary north-south line over your head) at local noon. But in the 17th century, how were you to know the time at Greenwich when you were in the ocean hundreds of miles away?

The obvious answer was to take an accurate clock on the ship, set to Greenwich Time before sailing, but that wasn't practical then since an accurate pendulum clock wouldn't work on a rolling ship. Pocket watches were being made but none were yet good enough for navigation at sea. Navigators and surveyors had turned to astronomy hoping for an answer.

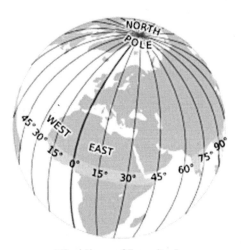

Meridians of Longitude

The Royal Observatory, Greenwich

During the course of the night the Moon appears to change its position, against the background of stars, by its own width every hour – like the hand of a clock moving across the dial. Astronomers knew that in theory the apparent position of the Moon could be used to find Greenwich Time anywhere in the world. This 'lunar distance method' needed a book of tables (later called the *Nautical Almanac*) to enable navigators to convert measurements of the Moon's position to Greenwich time, but in the mid-17th century the Nautical Almanac didn't exist. A major programme of astronomical measurement was needed to develop the tables.

In 1675, the King of England, Charles II, was persuaded to help and he put up £500 to establish an astronomical observatory, the Royal Observatory, duly designed and built for him in Greenwich Park by Sir Christopher Wren. John Flamsteed, the first Astronomer Royal, began work there but was an obsessive perfectionist and didn't want to share his observations prematurely. Little was published in his lifetime. There were various campaigns to educate navigators in 'best practice' but nobody was helping mariners to find longitude.

The Wreck of the Association

As late as 1707, 30 years after Flamsteed began work on the problem, a maritime disaster rocked the Royal Navy. Returning from the siege of Toulon with a fleet of 21 warships, Admiral Sir Cloudesley Shovell had been dogged by gales and bad weather. On the night of 22 October, the fleet approached the English Channel and Shovell believed he was safely west and at the latitude of Ushant on the Brittany coast. At 8 pm, Shovell's flagship, the *Association,* struck the Outer Gilstone Rock on the coast of the Scilly Isles. The *Association* quickly foundered, taking her crew of 900 with her. She was followed by the *Eagle*, the *Rumney* and the *Firebrand*. The *St George* and the *Phoenix* also struck but managed to get off.

The wreck of the *Association* 1707

Different accounts estimate that somewhere between 1400 and 2000 of the crews drowned including Cloudesley Shovell himself. The Admiral's body and those of his stepsons later washed ashore at Porthellick Cove on St Mary's, 11 km from the wreck.

Shovell was a long way from where he believed he was. The Scilly Isles are over 180 km north and maybe 60 km west of his presumed position, and, indeed, at the time, it seems the position of the isles themselves was poorly charted. The wreck also spawned several sensational stories including the claim that Shovell was alive when washed ashore and was murdered for his emerald ring. Colourful as they are, and often repeated, there is no hard evidence for these related tales.

In all likelihood the disaster did not itself trigger government action although it may have contributed to it. In any case, there is no doubt that the "wreck of the *Association*" was a graphic and terrible illustration of the perils at sea resulting from poor navigation.

The Longitude Act, 1714

Certainly, from about the time of the wreck in 1707, dissatisfaction with Flamsteed and concern for lack of progress on the longitude problem was growing. Work had begun earlier on the publication of Flamsteed's observations supervised by referees led by Isaac Newton, President of the Royal Society, but the work had stalled and relations between Flamsteed and Newton were deteriorating. In 1713, a determined campaign began to pressure the British Government to take action.

In 1714, almost 40 years after Flamsteed had started the work, the Government resolved to wait no longer for Greenwich to produce a solution. With the Longitude Act, they offered a reward of £20,000 to anyone proposing an accurate, 'practicable and useful' way of finding longitude at sea. This was a fabulous sum of money – over £6 million in modern buying power (if you were to spend it on beer).

A group of Commissioners known as the Board of Longitude was appointed to administer the reward. Now many strange and wondrous ideas were proposed but none took the money. The astronomers at Greenwich soldiered on. Flamsteed died at the end of 1719 and was replaced by the great Edmond Halley of comet fame.

Harrison's Longitude

Halley had much work left to do. When he'd been at Greenwich nearly 10 years, the Nautical Almanac was still out of reach. Then around 1730, a man appeared at the door of the Observatory saying he knew how to make a clock that would keep accurate time on a ship at sea. Such a 'sea clock' or 'marine timekeeper' could always show the navigator Greenwich Time and seemed to offer a much simpler answer to finding longitude than did astronomy.

The man who knocked on Halley's door was named John Harrison. All who have read Dava Sobel's enthralling account *'Longitude – the true story of a lone genius who solved the greatest scientific problem of his time'* will know how Harrison's visit to Greenwich began a struggle lasting over 40 years as he laboured to perfect his timekeepers and then fought to claim the

Longitude reward. This section provides a summary of the Harrison story. The interested reader will find more detail in the Appendix.

Harrison was self-taught with no university education; his craftsmanship was superb and his design ideas were highly innovative. In over 30 years, he built a series of four breath-taking clocks preserved for all to see at the Royal Observatory in Greenwich. The first three, now known as H1, H2 and H3, are large machines of brass and steel. Each stands roughly 60 cm tall (2 feet) and weigh between 30 and 47 kg (66 lbs and 103 lbs).

Harrison obtained a loan of money from England's best clockmaker and worked at home in Lincolnshire for 6 years building H1. After a promising test at sea, he borrowed more money, this time from the Board of Longitude, and moved to London. Helped by craftsmen in London he took just under 3 years to make H2, an improved version. Then he realised the design of H1 and H2 was flawed.

In 1741, he embarked on H3, his 'curious 3rd machine', with several innovations some of which we still use today. Eventually, Harrison toiled almost 20 years on H3 but failed to make it run to his satisfaction.

He resolved instead to make some watches – a watch with a fast-beating balance would be much less affected by the motion of the ship. The result in 1759 was H4 – a large watch about 125 mm (5 inches) in diameter, weighing about 1.4 kg (3 lbs).

H4 was taken twice to be tested on voyages to the West Indies by Harrison's son William. On the 1st voyage in 1761-2, the watch performed much better than required by the Act and John (now almost 70 years old) at last claimed the £20,000 reward. He was refused – the Board didn't know if copies (essential for the method to be available to all) would be possible, and also the astronomers, anxious to complete their work on the Almanac, lobbied against rewarding the watch.

The Board demanded a second trial and in 1764 William took the watch to Barbados and showed it was running even better – it performed three times better than required by the Act, a fantastic achievement.

The Board now offered half the reward, a huge sum, but John was not satisfied. He demanded the full amount and clashed with the Board. It was not to be for another 9 years after bitter argument and feuding with the Board that John was to see the full £20,000.

In 1765, for reluctantly disclosing the design of H4, John was at last granted £10,000. He was now a rich man, but to win the remaining £10,000 the Board demanded that he personally should make two copies of the watch. Also they required him to hand-over the original, H4, which they gave to another watchmaker, Larcum Kendall, to make a separate copy (of which more later).

John was then over 70 years old but by 1770 he had completed one copy, known as H5 (now in the collection of the Clockmakers Company). John's bad-tempered exchanges with the Board had convinced him that he would get no further satisfaction there and, with little time left to him, he approached the king, George III, who loved science and technology. The king took his side and with his help Harrison appealed directly to the British Parliament. In June 1773, by Act of Parliament, John Harrison received the rest of the money. He was 80 years old. Three years later, he was dead.

Later called 'marine chronometers', the successors of H4 would always show the time at home, say at Greenwich. The time difference between local time and Greenwich Time would tell you longitude – distance east or west from Greenwich. The Harrisons had discovered the longitude.

The astronomers at Greenwich didn't give up. In 1766, the 5th Astronomer Royal, Nevil Maskelyne, at last published the 1st edition of the *Nautical Almanac and Astronomical Ephemeris*. A mariner would use a *sextant* to measure the altitude of the Moon and the angle between the Moon and a nearby bright star. With around 30 minutes of calculation, the navigator could then use the Almanac's tables to convert the Moon's position to Greenwich Time. Navigators now had a choice of two methods to find longitude – by 'lunars' or by 'chronometer'.

So, let us return to the South Pacific in 1767. Did Carteret have a marine timekeeper? Certainly not – H4 was back from Barbados before Carteret sailed but the Board wouldn't permit H4 to leave the country again; H5 was not ready until 1770. Did Carteret have the Nautical Almanac needed to find longitude by lunars? Apparently not – Captain Cook was among the earliest to have one for his 1st voyage which sailed in 1768.

The mariner and author HG Mowat reviewed two logs from Carteret's voyage – Carteret's own *Journal* and a daily log book by Kerton, a member of the crew. Mowat confirms – "The *Swallow* had no chronometer and for that matter neither did the other two ships nor since no lunars were observed the longitude was determined by dead reckoning."[13] On the *Swallow,* "navigational instruments were limited to the compass and quadrant... It was the time-honoured method of log, lead and lookout"[14].

Carteret found his longitude 'by account' – he used dead reckoning: an estimate of his speed and course to do a calculation from his last position.

Now, thanks to Harrison (not forgetting the astronomers from Flamsteed to Maskelyne), the explorers and adventurers who followed Carteret could be better equipped. The stage was set for Larcum Kendall, James Cook and William Bligh.

---

[13] HG Mowat, Captain Carteret and the voyage of the Swallow 1776-79, p20
[14] Ibid, p34-35

Chapter 3
Larcum Kendall
By Mike Dryland

Enter Larcum Kendall. A London watchmaker of Furnival's Inn Court, we first find him in the story in 1765 at John Harrison's disclosure of H4's design. By then Kendall had clearly established himself with a first-rate reputation. He was one of three watchmakers among the six experts at the disclosure.

Following the disclosure of H4's design, Harrison now began to make his own copy (H5), and the Board decided to commission another from a different maker. In May 1767, on Harrison's recommendation, Larcum Kendall was chosen (a great honour), given the watch H4 and asked to make a copy. Kendall was to be paid £450 with half paid in advance. Kendall set about this and completed the task 2½ years later. The result is now known as K1, Kendall-1.

We don't know a great deal about Kendall. He was born into a Quaker family in Charlbury, Oxford in 1719. By 1735, we find him apprenticed in London to one John Jefferys.

We know Jefferys was a close associate of John Harrison, maybe introduced to him through George Graham. It seems possible that Jefferys had assisted the Harrisons now and then since their move to London in 1736, and in 1753 Jefferys was chosen by Harrison to construct a pocket watch to Harrison's own design. The 'Jefferys Watch' contained many of Harrison's innovations and its excellent performance gave Harrison the confidence to continue his work.

Kendall, in Jefferys' employ, would also have known the Harrisons. At the end of his apprenticeship in 1742, Kendall set up his own business. He did work for George Graham making complex parts, but few complete watches are now known bearing

Kendall's signature – there is one in the collection of the Worshipful Company of Clockmakers in London. After Jefferys died in 1754, Kendall probably worked closely with Harrison. We certainly suppose that he was an important associate during the construction of H4 from 1755 to 1760.

Kendall began work on K1 in May 1767 and finished in January 1770. K1 is an almost exact copy of H4. Externally, there are two small differences – the shape of the bow, and two screw heads visible on the dial. Internally, the engraving on the plates differs from H4 and, if anything, is more beautiful and elaborate than the original. William Harrison was pleased to concede that the workmanship in K1 was superior to his father's in H4. Kendall was paid a bonus of £50, making a total of £500 for K1 – a large sum, call it £30,000 in modern values.

Larcum Kendall's Timekeeper K1 – 1769

A lot rested on K1. Success in use on a long voyage under respected leadership would likely influence the Board of Longitude to look upon Harrison's claim favourably.

Captain James Cook had a high reputation following his first voyage in the *Endeavour*, which had explored the Pacific and the east coast of 'New South Wales' (Australia), where he confidently claimed the entire continent for Britain. There had been no marine timekeepers available for Cook's 1st voyage – his superb navigation was by 'lunars' and he took early copies of the Nautical Almanac.

Cook now prepared for a second voyage of discovery, this time with two ships. K1 came on board the *Resolution* in April 1772 with astronomer William Wales, while a second astronomer, William Bayley, joined the *Adventure*. The Board of Longitude demanded real discipline in the tests of the K1 timekeeper and there could be no room for tampering. K1 was contained in a specially made box with three locks and located in the great cabin. It was wound daily at noon in the presence of the three key-holder witnesses.

During a five month trip around New Zealand and to the edge of the Antarctic, K1 never lost more than eight seconds a day and averaged a loss of just 3 seconds, which was remarkable. Cook had an enquiring mind but was initially cautious about timekeepers. Later, he was converted and referred to K1 as "Our never failing guide, the watch" and "Our trusty friend, the watch". He and others used different names for the watch including "timekeeper", "time piece" and even "watch machine".

The master of the *Resolution* on Cook's second voyage was John Gilbert who claimed that K1 was "The greatest piece of mechanism the world has ever seen".

Kendall's K1 was of such a high quality that the Board enquired whether he could make more of them and train more people. Kendall thought Harrison's design was too complex and costly to produce in quantity. He offered to make a new watch to a simplified design for £200, less than half the price of K1.

The Board gave Kendall the order in May 1770 and he immediately started work, completing his new design two years later. This was K2, still a large watch weighing 1343g and measuring 165mm by 128mm by 51mm. K2 however looks quite different to H4. The long minute hand reaches to the edge of the main dial; seconds and hours have separate subsidiary dials.

Costs were saved by omitting some important parts of Harrison's mechanism. "It did not take long to ascertain that in order to simplify Harrison's design, and thus construct it for £200, that Kendall had committed the cardinal error of dispensing with the train remontoire". [15] (A 'remontoire' is a part of the watch's mechanism that evens-out the delivery of power to the escapement).

Larcum Kendall's Timekeeper K2 – 1771

In 1773 K2 was issued to Captain Constantine Phipps for a voyage of exploration to the Arctic, and that is where our story really starts in the next chapter.

---

[15] Peter Amis 'The Bounty Timekeeper', The Horological Journal, December 1957

Let us first complete the account of Kendall's work. He was asked by the Board to make a third watch, now called K3, completed in 1774 at a cost of just £100. The movement of K3 is similar to K2 but has a modified design of mechanism. Costs were reduced – "K3 is practically identical to K2, except in the escapement, which has two coaxial crown-wheels, whose teeth engage with a single ruby pallet placed between them".[16]

Externally, K3 appears very different – it has three small dials, one each for hours, minutes and seconds. Like K2, K3 was also valued for finding longitude at sea but didn't measure up to the original H4/K1.

Larcum Kendall's Timekeeper K3 – 1774

The movement is inscribed 'Larcum Kendall, London, 1774'. The diameter of the watch is 102 mm. The timekeeper is now in an octagonal mahogany wooden box which was

---

[16] Rupert T Gould ' The Marine Chronometer, its History and Development' The Antique Collectors' Club 2013

originally gimballed in an outer box. The box was made by John Roger Arnold in 1802.

K3 was quickly put to use. A third voyage of exploration to the Pacific was being planned by the Admiralty and Cook was the obvious leader. Cook was reluctant, wanting to spend more time with his family. On the other hand, his responsibilities ashore weren't challenging. He later wrote to John Walker: "the limits of Greenwich Hospital which are far too small for an active mind like mine." Cook allowed himself to be persuaded in early 1776 to lead his 3rd and final voyage.

It was a voyage designed to fulfil a number of objectives. The main quest was to follow up earlier attempts to discover the fabled ice-free Northwest Passage which might allow shipping to pass directly between the Pacific and Atlantic oceans through the Arctic Ocean north of North America.

In 1728, Vitus Bering, a Swede working for Russia, had shown that a strait did exist, separating Asia from America. The Admiralty considered that ideally the search for a passage should be undertaken from both sides with the Russians from the east and the British from the west. Here though was an opportunity for Cook to search from the Pacific.

The *Resolution* would be accompanied by another converted Whitby collier, the *Discovery*, under Captain Charles Clerke. Kendall's precious timekeeper K1 was allocated to the *Resolution* and the new K3 to the *Discovery*. Cook appointed a 22-year-old up-and-coming master by the name of William Bligh on the *Resolution*. William Bayley, the astronomer from the previous voyage, was reappointed to serve on the *Discovery*.

The *Resolution* sailed in July 1776 and the *Discovery* followed a few weeks later, both heading for Cape Town. In late January 1777 the fleet reached Van Diemen's Land (Tasmania) in Australia and anchored in Adventure Bay taking on wood, water and any animal fodder available. William Bligh was using K1 on the *Resolution* and would probably have compared it with K3 from the *Discovery* when on shore, in the expedition's portable observatory.

Ten years later Bligh would be stopping again at the same place for the same reasons, but as captain of the *Bounty* with K2 on board.

New Zealand was next. The young artist John Webber made a name for himself with his prodigious sketches and paintings. Cook was island-hopping in the Pacific working his way northwards. The islands included Tonga, Tahiti and Hawaii.

Cook made one attempt to find the Northwest Passage, without success, running into a barrier of ice. He turned back south to Hawaii and tragedy. Cook was killed there on 14 February 1779.

On 26 April 1779, two months after Cook's death, K1 stopped working. It had run impeccably for nearly three years but suddenly came to a standstill. Captain Clerke on the *Resolution* checked that it had been wound correctly. By chance, there was a seaman on board called Benjamin Lyon who had been apprenticed to a watchmaker. Captain Clerke asked him to examine K1. He reported that dirt had jammed the mechanism. Cleaning and light oiling initially did the trick but soon the watch stopped again. Lyon built a new balance spring, an impressive achievement under the circumstances, but to no avail.

For a second attempt to see the fleet through the Bering Strait and Arctic Circle, K3 was transferred from the *Discovery* to the *Resolution*. Unfortunately, this attempt on the Northwest Passage also failed, so the fleet sailed for home.

In September 1780, driven north by bad weather, the small expedition arrived at the Orkney Islands, north of Scotland. The two precious timekeepers, K1 and K3, were sent ahead overland to Greenwich, and then dispatched to Larcum Kendall for repairs and cleaning.

The Board put all of Kendall's marine timekeepers to good use. On its return from Cook's tragic 3rd voyage, K1 was repaired and between 1787 and 1792 was used by Captain Arthur Phillip in command of the 'First Fleet' transporting convicts to establish the new settlement at Botany Bay, New South Wales. In 1793 it was loaned to Sir John Jervis and may have been on board his flagship *Victory* at the battle of Cape St. Vincent in 1797. Sir John didn't return K1 to the Board of Longitude until 1802 after which it finally retired from sea service.

After Cook, Kendall's 3rd marine watch K3 was loaned to Commodore John Elliot in *Romney*, then in 1791-95 sailed with Captain George Vancouver for his exploration of America's northwest coast where his efforts are remembered in many place names. On its return it was intended to serve with Matthew Flinders in *Investigator* in 1802 but was delayed in England and only caught up with Flinders after he had completed his great circumnavigational survey of Australia. K3 was pensioned-off in 1804 and kept at the Royal Observatory, Greenwich.

Each of Kendall's longitude watches took part in some of the most exciting adventures of the period, and any one of them could form the basis for a great tale. All three are now in the collection of the National Maritime Museum at Greenwich.

But this book is the story of Kendall's second watch, K2, and the lives and places it touched.

While Cook was exploring in the Pacific, Kendall's K2 had already begun its adventures starting with its maiden voyage towards the North Pole commanded by Captain Phipps and accompanied by young midshipman Horatio Nelson.

Chapter 4
Captain Phipps – Towards the North Pole
1773 K2 1st Voyage

The South Winds say – "Delay! Delay!"
The Soft Winds say – "O Stay! O Stay!"
And be thou lulled as we will;
Then go not forth to the dreary North,
Where the winds and the hearts are chill!

Harp of St Hilda. Richard Winter.

The dream of discovering a North West Passage between the Atlantic and Pacific oceans began in the 16th century once the Pacific and Southern hemispheres were opened up to the world. Spitsbergen had been discovered to the North and was being profitably used by Dutch, British and French whalers.

Lord Sandwich proposed to King George III a summer expedition for a new voyage of discovery "to try how far navigation was practicable towards the North Pole". Objectives included exploring the unknown oceans over 80° and seeking the elusive North West Passage to the Pacific. The King approved the proposal and the Admiralty ensured the expedition was well equipped with two sturdy vessels.

The leader would be Captain Constantine John Phipps Mulgrave RN, known as Captain Phipps who received his commission on 19 April 1773. He would sail in a converted bomb vessel, the *Racehorse*, while the supporting ship was another bomb vessel called the *Carcass* under Captain Skeffington Lutwidge.

The *Racehorse* was slightly bigger at 385 tons compared to the 309 tons of the *Carcass*. Bomb boats were usually specifically built gun vessels strengthened to carry heavy mortars, which could lob weighty explosive bombs landwards. They could also be converted sloops. On this voyage, the strength was needed to withstand crushing ice floes, so the Admiralty proposed "that the bottoms of the said sloops may be doubled; their bows fortified by breasthooks and sleepers"[17].

Phipps heard about the expedition at the Royal Society and put himself forward to Lord Sandwich. Phipps was impressed by the thoughtfulness of the Admiralty's meticulous planning of this voyage. In his 1773 journal addressed to the King, he noted, "It was foreseen that one or both of the ships might be sacrificed in the prosecution of the undertaking; the boats for each ship, on any emergency could transport the whole crew." Phipps continued, "Everything which could tend to promote the security, health and convenience of the ship's companies, was granted."

Great attention was paid to the latest navigational instruments. "The Board of Longitude sent two 'watch machines' for keeping the longitude by difference of time; one constructed by Mr Kendall (K2) on Mr Harrison's principles and the other by Mr Arnold. I had also a pocket watch constructed by Mr. Arnold, by which I kept the longitude to a degree of exactitude beyond what I could have expected; the watch having varied…only 2' 40" in 128 days."[18]

The Board also arranged for Mr Israel Lyons to join the expedition as an astronomer and mathematician "to make nautical and astronomical observations and to make trial of some Longitude Watches"[19]. This was a real coup since he had worked for the Board of Longitude with Nevil Maskelyne helping to produce the Nautical Almanac tables.

---

[17] ARCTIC Vol. 37, p404 / "Point in Geography", Ann Savours, NMM. (ARC/SAV)
[18] Phipps's Journal 1773, p12. "Voyage towards the North Pole" (PHI)
[19] ARC/SAV, p408

Phipps made a point of thanking his good friend the naturalist Joseph Banks "for very full instructions in the branch of natural history"[20].

The two Longitude watches, or timekeepers, were heavily guarded, "Mr Arnold's was suspended in gimbals, but Mr Kendall's was laid between two cushions which quite filled up the box". Phipps added, "The boxes were screwed down to the shelves of the cabin, and each had three locks, one key kept by the captain, another by the first lieutenant and the third by myself." Kendall's K2 sailed on the *Racehorse* while Arnold's timekeeper was on the *Carcass*.

They were wound every noon and then compared with Phipps's personal watch. "They (the timekeepers) stopped twice in the voyage, owing to their being run down. It was easy to know how long each had stopped from the others still going; this time is allowed for in the table of mean time at Greenwich."

It is understandable that Phipps particularly valued his Arnold pocket watch since it was so convenient to handle and take ashore since the "other timekeepers could not be safely moved' and 'the longitude was not very different from the truth"[21]. Unlike some naval commanders, Phipps was very much an enthusiastic 'hands on' officer when it came to assessing new nautical navigational instruments.

On 30 May 1773, the *Carcass* under Captain Lutwidge joined the *Racehorse* under the overall command of Captain Phipps at the Nore on the Thames. On 2 June, Mr Arnold turned up to regulate his timekeeper on the *Carcass*, which had stopped, "for want of being…wound up". Also, "Mr Lyons landed with an Astronomical Quadrant at Sheerness fort".

The journey took them up the east coast and on 5 June the ships briefly stopped at Orford Castle in Suffolk. Next day the expedition passed Southwold while sailing to Scarborough on 9 June, before anchoring in Robin Hood's Bay on the way to Whitby.

Both ships had been supplied with a freshwater apparatus designed by Dr Irving for distilling pure fresh water from the sea,

---

[20] PHI, p12
[21] Ibid, p229

"with great successes. Some 34–40 gallons of additional drinking water could be produced per day from each unit"[22].

Since neither of the leaders had sailed in Arctic waters, the Admiralty had thoughtfully employed four sailors from Greenland to provide two seasoned pilots for each ship.

The ships continued on a general northerly direction, depending on winds. On 14 June, some Shetland fishing boats appeared, bearing fresh fish. By mean of two lunar observations, the *Racehorse* was in longitude 2° 16' 45". At noon, the latitude was 60° 16' 45". [23]

Midshipman Thomas Floyd was on the *Carcass* officer's list but appeared to sail on the *Racehorse* and was keeping his own narrative. He wrote when near the Shetlands, "Here we might remark on the excellence of Harrison and Arnold's time pieces to which the astronomers continually referred, and which gave us longitude." Possibly, K2 was confused with Kendall's K1, a copy of Harrison's H4.[24]

It was occasionally foggy when Phipps "could not see the *Carcass* but heard her answer the signals for keeping company". On 20 June, Phipps on the *Racehorse* was "trying to get soundings at much greater depths than I believe had ever been attempted before. I sounded with a very heavy lead the depth of 780 fathoms, without getting ground".

Another scientific experiment, with which they were charged, was to take regular water temperature checks by 'Lord Cavendish's thermometer' at different depths; as deep as 118 fathoms.

On 27 June 1773, latitude 74° 26', "We were in the evening, by all our reckonings, in the latitude of the South part of Spitsbergen without any appearance of ice or land." On 29, they stood close to land, "The coast appeared to be neither habitable nor accessible." Other parts "were covered in snow appearing even above the clouds".

Running along the West coast of Spitsbergen, the *Racehorse* "stood in a small bay southward of Magdalena and Hamburger

---

[22] Ibid, p222

[23] Ibid, p25

[24] Thomas Floyd, A Midshipman's Narrative of Phipps's Polar Voyage 1773

Bay" while sending out a boat for water. Early next morning on 5 July, a master from a Greenland ship informed Phipps that ice was within ten leagues of Hakluyt's Headland to the North West. Phipps gave orders to steer there, "intending to go north from hence, till circumstances obliged me to alter my course".

Later that day ice was found accompanied by fog but the ice became thicker on 6 June as the weather improved. On 7, the ice "appeared to be close all 'round", but there were hopes for an opening northwards. "The *Carcass* was very close but not answering her helm well."

Although the *Carcass* had difficulty keeping up with the *Racehorse*, there was contact and discussion with the pilots about their icy position as they continued to seek any openings. A SW wind on 9 July helped them "stood to the Westward" and make some northwards gains enabling an observation latitude fix of 81° 52'. This appears to be the most northerly point of the expedition.

There was more 'impenetrable ice' on the 10th so Phipps stood to the east to ascertain whether the ice was joined to Spitsbergen. On the 13th, they anchored for five days at Clove Cliff, their most northern point. They spent their time on the ice carrying out scientific tasks and testing the pendulum clock by Lyons, while some of the crew went hunting and servicing the ships.

The ships sailed again on 18 July but on the 19th in 20 fathoms, "we found ourselves nearly in the same place where we had twice been stopped"[25]. On the 23rd, they were striking loose ice, seven leagues from Hakluyt's Head Land. "The ships had been so well strengthened, that they received no damage."

Over the next few days, they briefly landed on Moffen Island for some observations and hunting, before moving on. On 29 July, they were near the Waygat's Straits near Low Island. Phipps wrote, "Having little wind, two of our officers went with a boat in pursuit of some sea horses, and afterwards to the low island." On the way back to the *Racehorse*, "they fired at, and wounded, a sea horse"[26].

---

[25] PHI, p48
[26] Ibid, p58

These 'sea horses' were walruses which are renowned for getting upset if stabbed or shot. The wounded walrus dived and "brought up with it a number of others". They attacked the boat tearing an oar from a man while also threatening to overturn the vessel. Fortunately, a boat from the *Carcass* arrived and joined the battle, compelling the walruses to disperse.

View of the *Racehorse* and *Carcass*, August 7th, 1773

The officer on the rescuing boat from the *Carcass* was a young 14-year-old midshipman, Horatio Nelson.[27] The connection for Nelson's appointment was that Lutwidge had served under Captain Maurice Suckling who was Nelson's uncle. Lutwidge must have been happy to do a favour for his earlier commander. Nelson was later promoted to coxswain and put in charge of the ship's cutter.

The incident of Nelson rescuing the *Racehorse* boat under attack from enraged walruses is well documented, but he had another encounter with dangerous wild life, which is even more famous.

One night during mid-watch, Nelson persuaded a midshipman colleague to leave his post and join him on the ice

[27]ARC/SAV, p416. Conway 1906, p281

and snow to hunt for a 'white bear'. Although it was about 4 am, it was as clear as daylight at that latitude. A light fog hid their disappearance but when it lifted, Captain Lutwidge and officers could see the two youngsters close to a chasm tackling a large polar bear on the other side. Apparently, the musket misfired and Nelson was seen swinging it by the muzzle to hit the bear with the musket butt.

The two were clearly in danger and the Captain sent a signal to return immediately, which was obeyed by the companion but ignored by the spirited Nelson. Perhaps Horatio was honing his later skills of 'turning a blind eye'. After his gun failed, Nelson said to his companion before he left, "Never mind, do let me get a blow at this devil with the butt end of my musket, and we shall have him." Lutwidge ordered cannon fire, which caused the hostile polar bear to flee.

The Captain understandably gave Midshipman Nelson a strong dressing down for conduct unworthy of his office and demanded the reason. "Sir, I wished to kill the bear, that I might carry the skin to my father".[28]

The prime evidence appears to be largely anecdotal by Captain Lutwidge who related it at social gatherings from 1800, well after Nelson was famous and again after 1809, when the hero was dead. This incident inspired the famous heroic painting by Richard Westall, which is in a collection held by Royal Museums Greenwich.

Nelson was lucky, since Lutwidge could have destroyed his career there and then for leaving his post. The close family connections must have helped but kindly Lutwidge must have also been impressed, since he refrained from making it a major issue. Nelson didn't appear to write about this adventure but later referred to Lutwidge as that good old man.[29]

Lord Sandwich's instructions had been: "If you find it impracticable to proceed up to, or near the Pole, you are...to leave those seas so timely as to secure your return to the Nore before the winter sets in." The instructions to Captain Phipps were crystal clear.

---

[28] ARC/SAV, p416. R Southey, "Life of H. Nelson", p8
[29] John Sugden, Dream of Glory, p66

On 31 July, while the crew happily played leap-frog on the ice, the Greenland pilots were less cheerful, "being much further north and east than they had ever been and the season advancing, they seemed alarmed at being beset". They knew danger. A conference was called by Phipps and "it was unanimously agreed that the position was hopeless".

5 August 1773, Phipps wrote, "I sent Mr Walden, one of the midshipmen, with two pilots to an island about twelve miles off, which I have distinguished in the charts by the name of Walden Island to see where the open water lay." On the 6th, he was getting more worried and ordered canvas bread bags packed into two launches on the ice, in case of abandoning ships.

On 7 August, about 40 officers and men started dragging the launches over the ice. The launch from the *Carcass* was their four oared cutter commanded by Nelson. The crews were anxiously looking for breaks in the closing ice. About noon, the water by the ships seemed a bit more open.

Phipps reported on the 9th, "A thick fog in the morning. We moved the ship a little through some very small openings. In the afternoon, upon it clearing up, we were agreeably surprised to find the ships had driven much more than we could have expected to the westward."

Next day brought huge relief. "About noon, we had got her through the ice and out to sea." On the 11th, "Came to an anchor in the harbour of Smeerenberg (near Hakluyt's Headland) to refresh our people after their fatigues. The Dutch ships still resort to this place for the later season of the whale fishing"[30].

Conditions continued to improve as they made their way south and Phipps wrote, "In steering southward, we soon found the weather grew milder, or rather our feelings warm." On 24 August, "we saw Jupiter; the sight of a star was now almost as an extraordinary phenomena as the sun at midnight within the Arctic Circle".

On 4 September, Phipps attempted a deep water sounding in a calm sea and it struck ground at six hundred and eighty three fathoms. The bottom was "a fine soft blue clay". The expedition passed by the Shetlands and continued south to Orford, where they anchored on 24 September 1773.

---

[30] PHI, p65–69

There have been criticisms of Phipps's expedition, partly because they did not reach the North Pole, which was in fact impossible. Their instructions were: "a voyage towards the North Pole". The ships not only reached 10 degrees from the Pole which was probably the most northern position by western sailors to date, but they successfully escaped from deadly ice traps. Finding the North West Passage to the Pacific from the Atlantic was always a longer term objective.

Any expedition involving Joseph Banks would include natural science objectives in both botany and zoology. Information and some specimens were brought back to Britain about the 'white bear', seals, whale foetuses, birds (particularly the Ivory Gull) Arctic foxes, shells, flora, mosses, lichens and even floating tree trunks.

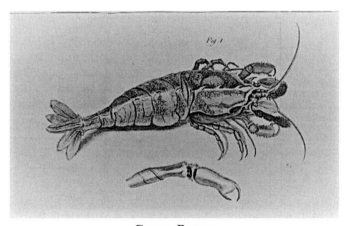

Cancer Boreas

In addition, the expedition made a great many scientific observations, including water temperatures at different depths, winds and currents. The distillation of sea water into drinking water was a real success. Navigational tools included using pendulum clocks for on-shore work, astronomical quadrants, the 1767 nautical almanac, different sextants and early Kendall and Arnold chronometers, for establishing the ship's position in accordance with the instructions below.

Israel Lyons and the Timekeepers

The direct instruction to Israel Lyons had been clear, "You are to wind up the watches every day as soon after noon as you can conveniently, and compare them together and set down the respective times; and you to note also the times of the Watches when the Sun's Morning and Afternoon Altitudes, or the distances of the moon from the Sun and fixt stars are observed; and to compute the Longitude, resulting from the comparison of the watches, with the apparent time of the Day inferred from the morning and afternoon Altitudes of the Sun."[31]

A daily comparison was taken comparing the Kendall and Arnold time pieces with the personal pocket watch belonging to Phipps both on shore and on the moving ships. Lyons was on the *Racehorse* with K2 and Phipps's personal Arnold pocket watch, while the Arnold time piece was on the *Carcass*. They regularly signalled comparative readings between the ships.

Lyons noted that the two timekeepers were of a size more convenient than earlier models but the Arnold pocket watch was 'exceedingly useful' for observations on land. There were constant comparisons at Noon but it appears the small Arnold pocket watch was preferred for both accuracy and convenience. The Kendall K2 appeared to be next best, but they noted Mr Arnold's larger timekeeper was very different when returning from Spitsbergen, "owing probably to the balance spring being rusty, when it was opened by the Royal Observatory at Greenwich"[32].

Unlike K1, which was a great success on Cook's voyages, K2 was deliberately built to a lower, cheaper specification, which showed on its first active voyage.

After disembarking, Phipps went off with his precious pocket watch while the two timepieces were returned to the Royal Observatory. The Arnold was found to have a rusty spring. K2 was examined and submitted to further checks before its next challenging voyage.

---

[31] PHI, Appendix p222
[32] Ibid, p231

This valuable expedition was a close shave. The first active voyage of K2 was very nearly the last. Midshipman Thomas Floyd, a colleague of Midshipman Nelson, recorded in his narrative, "If the wind had not changed more to the Northwards, destruction would have been inevitable."[33]

---

[33] Thomas Floyd Narrative

Chapter 5
Captain Vandeput – American Revolution
1775 K2 2nd Voyage

Captain Phipps reported to the Admiralty on his return from the Arctic after anchoring in Orford, Suffolk. The two marine time-pieces were returned by hand to the Royal Observatory in Greenwich for intensive checking before being allocated to other expeditions. Kendall's K2 did not have long to wait, since trouble was brewing in the North American colonies, where a revolutionary war was looming.

Asia was a new ship, launched in March 1764 in Portsmouth. It was a substantial 1364 tonnes, 64-gun 3rd rate 'ship of the line'. Such a ship would be furnished with full navigational equipment, so a range of instruments including K2 were allocated to it. K2 had survived near destruction in Arctic ice fields on its maiden voyage, only to face unknown dramas and dangers in a hostile war zone on the 2nd voyage.

Captain George Vandeput was the illegitimate son of a baronet who probably helped him gain his first position in 1759 as a midshipman. Young Vandeput subsequently proved himself by commanding small sloops and then as post captain on a number of frigates.[34]

He already had some experience of North American waters since he had been a midshipman on *Neptune*, stationed in the St Lawrence River where he was promoted to lieutenant. The

---

[34] Oxford Dictionary of National Biography

Admiralty must have thought highly of him since they offered him command of the *Asia* well before it was launched.[35]

After an uneventful Atlantic crossing, *Asia* equipped with K2, entered Boston Harbour in early January 1775 and joined *Somerset* and *Boyne* in landing an initial 460 marines to support General Gage. Another 700 marines were later landed to bolster Major John Pitcairn before fighting at Lexington, Concorde, Bunker's and Breed's Hill.

Major Pitcairn was a popular Scottish officer who found himself in Boston in December 1774 where his first task was to train a bunch of raw and ill-equipped recruits into a fighting unit.

On 19 April 1775, General Gage, who was the overall regional British army commander, sent Major Pitcairn to accompany Colonel Smith to seize and destroy supplies and arms stores of the Provincial Congress. In an imaginative night attack, the British troops went up the Charles River by boat and disembarked at Cambridge for the Concord and Lexington road.

Unbeknown to the advancing troops, patriot Paul Revere and friends on horseback had already passed the word around that "the British are coming". Bells were ringing, guns firing and Charleston North church had been primed to light one lantern if the British came 'by land' and two if 'by sea'.

---

[35] HMS Asia, Jesse Russell, Ronald Cohn, p5

Paul Revere's Ride

And yet, through the gloom and the light,
The fate of a nation was riding that night;
And the spark struck out by that steed in his flight, Kindled
the land into flame with its heat.

(Longfellow)

Major Pitcairn and his marines were rapidly sent ahead to take control of Lexington and any bridges, before moving on to Concord. Major Pitcairn arrived in Lexington at 5 am only to find the local militia out in force. On the back of his horse, he boldly remonstrated with the militia, "Disperse you rebels. Throw down your arms and instantly disperse."[36]

---

[36] British Battles, James Grant, 1897, p19

Major Pitcairn Entering Lexington

The rebels appeared to disperse, but some claim that irregular patriots fired individual shots, provoking the troops to fire back. The troops moved on to Concord and successfully destroyed the ordnance and stores, although this was later denied.

Did Major Pitcairn 'fire the first shot' in this war? His report of 26 April to General Gage included, "rebels who had jumped over the wall fired four or five shots at the soldiers". Two lines in the first verse of Emerson's famous 1837 Concord Hymn appear to imply the patriots fired the first shot:

"Here once the embattled farmers stood
and fired the shot heard 'round the world."

However, Connecticut reports confirm that when the rebels didn't disperse, the Major "rode a few yards, discharged his pistol, and brandished his sword…" There can be little doubt that a 'Pitcairn Pistol' probably fired one of the first shots in the American Revolutionary War but it was aimed in the air.[37]

The return march back to Boston was a nightmare for the British troops. Many Massachusetts's militias had been roused

---

[37] History Connecticut, GH Hollister, p161

and were waiting in ambush. The troops by then also included Colonel Smith's contingent. Major Pitcairn's horse was wounded by two shots and seeing which way the battle was going, it had the sense to bolt and join the enemy. The saddlebag included a fine pair of pistols and these 'Pitcairn Pistols' are now displayed at a Lexington Museum.[38] The retreating British troops were relieved to see Boston again.

Major John Pitcairn, who then reported to General Clinton, was subsequently killed in the battle of Bunker's Hill while leading a charge of his marines attacking with fearsome bayonets fixed to their Brown Bess muskets. He was shouting "the day is ours" before being shot by Peter Salem, an African-American soldier patriot; another Pitcairn family tragedy. The Major knew by then about the death of his midshipman son Robert Pitcairn and that his family name was commemorated forever on a remote Pacific island.

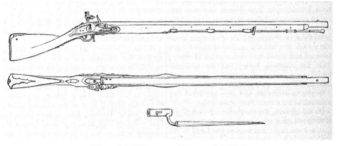

The Old Brown Bess of 1786

This was a classic Pyrrhic victory and the British General Sir Henry Clinton bemoaned, "It was a dear bought victory; another such would have ruined us."

As fate would have it, the K2-timekeeper was on the *Asia* when it was supporting Major Pitcairn's attack on Lexington,

---

[38] Munroe Tavern museum house, Lexington. The History of the Fife Pitcairns. NOTE: There are claims that the pistols' engraving wasn't that of the Pitcairn crest but owners were free to have any attractive and affordable design. It was the American Lexington militia who held the battle field and the ornate pistols were used by American General Israel Putnam throughout the war

and 14 years later, K2 would subsequently arrive on Pitcairn's Island for a very long stay, following the renowned *Bounty* mutiny.

The British were surprised by the size of the American 'citizen's army' and their weapon skills. Were these early battles an influence on the second amendment to the United States Constitution, "the people had the right to keep and bear arms"?

The *Asia* left Boston to sail into the troubled waters of New York harbour in May 1775. Captain Vandeput entered in his Log book "Moored in the East River New York abreast of the City"[39]. Indeed, much of the *Asia's* stay was either in New York or Boston harbour.

Some weeks were spent on provisioning and repairing the *Asia* before seeing action as part of Admiral Richard Lord Howe's fleet over a battery of guns on New York's waterfront. Following an intelligence gathering exercise on 24 August 1775, Vandeput logged:

"We sent our boat to lie under the Battery to make a Signal in case the Rebels should attempt to take away the guns…the boat made a Signal by Firing at Insurgents, several Vollies of small Arms was immediately Fired at the Boat by Persons on the Battery and killed one of the men. We then fired the Quarter and Upper Deck Guns and cleared the ship. All hands were hurried to Quarters…at 2 am several muskets were fired at the ship; immediately a broadside was fired with Vollies of small arms by the marines on the Poop…at day light we found that the Cannon that were mounted on the Battery had been taken away."[40]

New York was the second largest American city and as such, both sides wanted to hold it. From a naval perspective, New York was a potential trap. American author Barnet Schecter writes, "When the French joined the American cause and naval warfare became an important element of the Revolution, the British discovered that that the city's enormous and spectacular harbour was the worst possible location for a naval base."[41]

---

[39] Asia Log Book, p99.

[40] Ibid

[41] Barnet Schecter, Battle for New York, p5

Essentially, the harbour could entrap a fleet. Studies concluded that the "deep navigable waters around the City, could only be accessed by two very narrow and treacherous passageways. Most obvious was the shallow channel between Sandy Hook and the sand bar that extended north to Coney Island"[42].

The *Asia* was continuously at risk in New York. Even buying provisions from local suppliers could be fraught and the ship would keep on the move between Staten Island, East River, North River (Hudson), Rhode Island, Long Island, New London Lighthouse and wherever it saw fit.

On 7 April 1776, Captain Vandeput sent a sloop called *Savage* to a 'Watering Place' on Staten Island and "a Number of Rebels fired at them, killed two of her men and wounded three more"[43].

Since much of the maritime traffic was quite small, large ships such as the *Asia* would use smaller boats and sloops called 'tenders', to stop and search local traffic and they had some successes.[44]

Despatches from Admiral Shudham to the British Admiralty mentioned: "January 20, 1776, the *Asia* took the Schooner *James* in New York Harbour carrying provisions, Dry Goods, etc., to the rebel Camp." On 6 February 1776, the *Asia* captured a sloop under the command of Mr Murray on the North River with a cargo of Pig Iron.

When *Asia* was anchored off Gravesend Bay on Wednesday 3 July, it received a signal, "Landing the Troops. Manned Flat Boats".[45] This brief signal was another dangerous task for the King's navy. The *Asia* and flag ship *Eagle* were high profile targets for a resourceful enemy.

Fire and gunpowder were the weapons of war in the early battles near New York and using fire ships was inevitable in such close waters. Fire ships have been a weapon since classical Greek wars and the English had a notable success against the Spanish Armada.

---

[42] Ibid, p76

[43] Asia Log Book, p111

[44] Despatches of Molyneux Shuldmam, 1776, p246/7

[45] Asia Log Book, p115

Fire ships could be specially built but were usually obsolete wooden vessels loaded with flammable materials and either steered or allowed to drift by winds or tides towards enemy fleets. In closed harbours, they could create mayhem and panic for crews whose wooden and tarred ships were highly inflammable. If the fire ships had barrels of gunpowder under the decks, they became floating bombs. The skeleton crews on the attacking fire ships often had to be fast rowers, to survive.

An early attempt took place at night on 16 August 1776, when the patriot officer Nathan Hale arranged for men from his regiment to take two fire ships down the Hudson to burn British shipping.[46] One of the fire ships came across a small British bomb vessel, which was a tender to the *Rose,* a 20-gun 6th rate. Captain Wallace of *Rose* logged "saw…Rebel galleys, two of which prov'd to be fire vessels, our Tender being on Larbed Quarter, one of them fell Athwart (crossed her line) her on fire, which set the Tender Instantly in a Blaze"[47].

The second fire ship "fell athwart the Phoenix's Bow, which near set her on fire". There was little damage on the 44-gun 5th rate *Phoenix*, which cut its own rigging to escape the flames. *Rose* was safe, but the tender was lost, "Our people all got safe on board"[48]. Vigilance was vital.

Several months earlier, a British intelligence report dated 29 April 1776 had already informed the British Admiralty "have received information that the Rebels had an intention, of making an attempt to set the *Asia* on Fire by means of a number of vessels chained together, to be sent down upon an Ebb Tide, which runs very Strong"[49].

This attack on *Asia* was launched in mid-September 1776. Captain Vandeput's log book on 16 September confirmed "the Rebels sent 3 Fire Vessels down the North River (Hudson) which drove on Shore before they reached the shipping, during which time the cutter with all her furniture, broke adrift and was lost"[50]. Fortunately, K2 had as many lives as a cat.

---

[46] Barnet Schecter Battle NY, p114/5

[47] Journal Rose

[48] Journal Captain Wallace

[49] Despatches M Shuldman, p225

[50] Asia Log Book, p122

The fire attack on *Asia* was organised and carried out by Silas Talbot, who appears to have badly burnt himself. He became a much wounded and decorated American hero and a subsequent member of the House of Representatives.

Submarines in 1776 were another headache for the Royal Navy. They had warnings in earlier intelligence despatches about new American tactics on 16 November 1775. "The great news of the day with us is; now to destroy the (our) Navy. A certain Mr Bushnell has completed his Machine, and has been missing four weeks, returned this day week."

This dire warning continued,[51]

"It is conjectur'd that an attempt was made on the Asia, but proved unsuccessful – Return'd to New Haven in order to get a Pump (for the submarine) of a new construction which will soon be completed – when you may expect to see our Ships in Smoke."

David Bushnell was a mature student at Yale reading scientific and philosophical subjects. "Yale's fine library included standard 18th century scientific texts, so Bushnell had access to the best and latest information." These experiments included "methods to make gunpowder explode under water, terrifying onlookers"[52].

Although static diving bells had been around for centuries, an underwater vessel able to move up and down and steer in any direction had been the stuff of dreams. David Bushnell and his brother Isaac set to work in their home in Saybrook in mid-1775. The hull was oak and shaped like a large barrel strengthened with hoops. These skills were locally available but the mechanical parts needed innovative craftsmen. Clockmaker Isaac Doolittle, near Yale, helped with valves and pumps.

A front propeller was foot-driven to move the vessel forwards and backwards while a vertical propeller helped with ascent and descent. The 2 propellers were referred to as rowing oars. Air was, of course, critical and two snorkels were provided, but it was assumed that the vessel would generally be just below the surface where light, sight and air were present. Lead ballast

---

[51] Despatches M Shuldman, p225
[52] Connecticut History, Brenda Milkofsky

helped the submarine's balance. Navigation was by sight through the small windows and a compass.

The objective was to sink British ships. It carried a mine with 150 lbs of gunpowder, which could be deliberately set to explode at any time. Bushnell's team of two clockmakers "modified clockwork timing device to trigger a flintlock mechanism from a musket"[53]. The timing device would start ticking when the mine was released, hopefully giving enough time for the one-man crew to escape.

Although named the 'Turtle', it was also called the 'American Turtle', the 'Sea Monster' and 'Machine'. Later, floating mines were sometimes referred to as 'infernal machines'. Submarines create fear of an unknown, unseen threat.

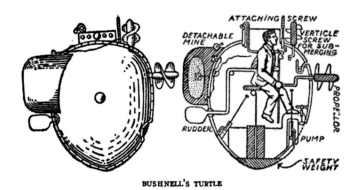

BUSHNELL'S TURTLE

Turtle Submarine c 1776

The target this time was not the *Asia* with K2, but the 64 gun *Eagle*, the British fleet's flagship and home to Admiral Richard Howe. Although Bushnell's brother Isaac had been trained on the Turtle, he became ill, so an inexperienced patriot Connecticut soldier, Sergeant Ezra Lee stepped in for some quick training and possible glory.

The attack on the night of 7 September 1776, took place a week before the fire ship attack on *Asia* in the same waters. The Turtle was towed out at night from New York City by whaling

---

[53] Ibid

boats. The intention was to release the submarine as near as possible to the *Eagle*, without being seen. The hapless Lee was dropped off 2 hours early to catch the right tide but he spent exhausting hours rowing his oars holding his position.

Ezra Lee later said, "When I rowed under the stern of the ship I could see men on deck and hear them talk, then I shut all doors, sunk down, and came up under the bottom of the ship, up with the screw against the bottom but found it would not enter."[54] The vertical screw seemed to be stopped by hard metal (not the hull's soft copper sheathing) so Lee had no choice but to abandon the attack, cut off the explosive magazine and retreat.

Lee said, "The magazine consequently drifted away from the ship, and when it exploded, did no harm to the British Admiral than give him a sad fright, as with the noise of an earthquake, it threw a column of water high into the air."[55]Lee was lucky since the explosion deterred a chasing boat and he escaped with the Turtle intact.

Later on, the Turtle carried out a couple of other attacks to little effect and was destroyed by the Royal Navy by chance when being transported. Bushnell continued with his floating clockwork mines with some success and some unintended civilian disasters, which were a spectre for the future 20th and 21st centuries when similar mines have led to 'collateral damage'. David Bushnell, 'Father of the Submarine', changed maritime warfare forever.

These incidents led to caution and nervousness by the British fleet in American harbours. Flotsam would often draw fire from the warships with no questions asked. Extreme caution probably saved the *Asia* and K2 from early destruction.

Although not apparently mentioned in Captain Vandeput's log book and letters, there are claims that one of the small British tenders used to search local boats for contraband came across a small coasting vessel stacked with gunpowder. The standard routine was to confiscate smuggled goods for Royal Navy use and either sink or release, the offending vessel.

Caution led Vandeput to order an arrested vessel to lie-off for the night, some distance from the *Asia*. During the night, one

[54] Ibid
[55] History Connecticut, GH Hollister, p272

of the prisoners in a terrified state approached a British guard on the small vessel, admitting that one of the barrels of gunpowder contained a musket piece, which would be fired by a clockwork mechanism at a set time.

The plan was based on the probability of the coastal vessel being stopped by the British who would load all the valuable gunpowder onto the Asia, before setting the vessel free.

There appears to have been a stand-off between two clocks. K2 on the *Asia* designed by clock maker Larcum Kendall would be telling the time at Greenwich, while the other clock designed by clock maker Isaac Doolittle, would be telling the time of a local Armageddon.

Sources appear vague as to what happened then, but probably the smuggling vessel was released. Considering the number and complexity of clever nautical tactics American patriots used against British coastal warships, this story is credible. Possibly, the British may have later felt they were duped.

Asia was moored at Prudence Island and then Newport Island in January 1777 before starting the journey home across the Atlantic. It subsequently moored in Portsmouth harbour in March 1777, before docking for repairs.

K2 had survived many risks on its 2nd voyage and returned to the peaceful safekeeping of the Royal Observatory in Greenwich. It would remain resting until 1781 when for its 3rd voyage it would be allocated to Rear Admiral George Digby who was the new Naval Commander of the American Station, where a bitter and bloody war was still raging.

Chapter 6
Admiral Digby – North American Station
1783 K2 3rd Voyage

Robert Digby was born on 20 December 1732, the son of the Hon. Edward Digby and his wife Charlotte Fox, but having two older brothers, he did not inherit his father's title. Nevertheless, Robert not only enjoyed a distinguished naval career, but also briefly became MP for Wells in Somerset and took his seat in the Commons.

It was traditional for younger aristocrat sons with little chance of a title, to seek careers in the church or the armed forces. Commissions could be bought in the army but not in the Royal Navy or Marines. 'Connections' probably helped Robert to enter the navy as a young midshipman.

This midshipman clearly enjoyed the navy, becoming a Captain of the frigate *Solebay* in 1755 when just twenty-three years old. He was evidently highly regarded, since the following year, Captain Robert Digby was posted to the 60 gun *Dunkirk* and a few years later promoted to the *Ramillies,* a 74-gun 'ship of the line'.

Further promotions followed. He became one of the two rear admirals in Rodney's fleet and was given command of the 96-gun *Prince George* and, following a series of battles with the French in the Seven Years war; he became 2nd in command of the Channel Fleet in 1779. In the same year, he was chosen to take under his wing as a midshipman, Prince William Henry, the 3rd son of King George III. This prince later became King William IV, known as the 'Sailor King', in 1830-37.

In 1781, Digby was appointed Admiral of the North American Station where the long and desperate war was coming to an end. King George's orders included an instruction to try to negotiate 'Home Rule' with the rebels, conditional on America remaining within the British Empire.

Digby's responsibilities included furthering the nautical use of new navigational tools. This particularly included Kendall's K2-timekeeper which, following its return with Captain Vandeput four years earlier, had remained in the Royal Observatory ever since.

This maritime watch was entrusted to Digby by the Board of Longitude but, being a busy man, he in turn gave the responsibility to Robert Waddington, for test and trial during his voyage. Waddington was a mathematician and assistant to Maskelyne. At the end of the voyage, Mr Waddington submitted his report to the Board, which began;

"On 7 July 1781, I received from one of Mr. Maskelyne's Assistants at Greenwich the second Timekeeper made by Mr Kendall for the Board of Longitude. It had not been going since the previous July, its mean Rate at that time was 17' per day when Fahrenheit thermometer read about 34°. In June 1780, its mean daily Rate of gaining had been 4' when the thermometer was from 64° to 70° high. In July 1781, I took it on board the *Prince George* after its daily rate of gain had been determined at Portsmouth Academy to be 2."[56]

Nevil Maskelyne Astronomer Royal and member of the Board of Longitude, was a strong advocate of the lunar distance method for finding longitude at sea. He was clearly also pursuing timekeeper technology by sending an expert with Admiral Digby, to use it in combination with the lunar method. It must have been Maskelyne's idea to assign Waddington to this voyage.

Since navigation was a vital skill for future officers, it was usual to teach and assist midshipmen in this subject while at sea. It must be highly likely that the gentleman from the Board of

---

[56] Waddington Report 1784 to Board of Longitude. Cambridge Digital Library (CDL)

Longitude would show Prince William Henry his timekeeper and discuss the merits and options. It is probable that K2 was held in royal hands.

Prince William Henry Serving as Midshipman on the *Prince George*

Admiral Digby had his hands full; he was moving into a complex war and diplomatic zone, so he was content to leave the tests and trials of K2 to Waddington. They crossed the Atlantic in Digby's 96-gun *Prince George*, arriving at Sandy Hook, an island off New York, on 24 August 1781 – to take command.

Digby discovered on arrival that his predecessor, Thomas Graves, was about to take his fleet to Yorktown to try for a second time to relieve the siege of Cornwallis and his army.

Admiral Digby was a courteous gentleman so he postponed his new command until Graves could grasp his chance of success. It was also a shrewd move since he couldn't be blamed for any disasters. Graves arrived a week too late and found the British had already surrendered to George Washington, which was effectively, the end of the active war.

The French fleet under de Grasse had by then moved on to the Caribbean while Graves returned to New York and resigned. The British admirals then focussed on defeating the French in the Caribbean, so all available warships were sent there. Digby remained in New York, changing his flagship to the *Lion* allowing the more powerful warship *Prince George* to join the West Indies Fleet under Sir Samuel Hood.[57]

Waddington was having a frustrating time since he was stuck on dry land in New York with his nautical navigational instruments. However, his luck changed when a captured French frigate the *L'Aigle* arrived and was sent to the Caribbean in late 1782. Waddington and K2 joined this ship and he mentioned in his report:

"My observation in N. York convinced me that its Rate of Gain was increasing – I attributed it to the coldness of the weather, because it had suffered the same Change in different states of the Atmosphere when in the Observatory in Greenwich, I determined it to be gaining 10" daily. We went to sea for 3 weeks and before our Return (allowing that Rate of gain) it made for the Lighthouse exactly – the thermometer in that interval was from 52° to 63° high."

Later, in November 1781, "I was ordered on Shore at N. York, where many Circumstances were so unfriendly to every kind of Astronomical Observations, that it would have been useless to have kept the Watch in Motion. It [K2] stood still from

---

[57] Naval Chronicles, Biographic memoirs, Vol 11

Nov '81 till Dec '82 when it went with me to the Indies in his Majesty's ship *L'Aigle*"[58].

Digby was aware of the young up and coming Captain Horatio Nelson who was then stationed in New York. Digby offered Nelson command of a local war ship, which had the potential of lucrative prize money. Young Nelson also had a Caribbean opportunity, so turned him down saying "the West Indies is the station for honour"[59].

The American Revolution was technically also the first American Civil War, which must be the worst kind of all wars. Patriots were called rebels and loyalists were called traitors, which divided homes, towns and cities. There were atrocities on both sides.

A number of British officers bemoaned this war against kith and kin, since they had fought together with American officers, including George Washington, against the French in the Seven Years War. Among them, General Sir William Howe came in for criticism in the early stages of the war for allowing the Continental army to escape from Long Island because he was desperate to come to an amicable solution.

General Howe carried this goodwill too far by having a long term American mistress, Mrs Betsey Loring. A local ballad by Francis Hopkinson in 1778 ran:

"Sir William he, snug as a flea,
Lay all this time a-snoring,
Nor dreamed of harm as he lay warm,
In bed with Mrs. Loring."[60]

Sniggering British army nicknames of her were 'The Sultana' and 'The Flashing Blonde'.

This personal relationship led to Howe granting his mistress's husband, Joshua Loring, the contract to supply food and supplies to patriot prisoners. This was a tragic decision since

---

[58] Waddington Report, Ibid CDL
[59] Robert Southey, The Life of Lord Nelson, p18
[60] Propaganda by Hopkinson, signed Declaration of Independence

much of the money seemed to stay in the husband's pocket, while rebel prisoners often starved in prison ships.[61]

Admiral Digby arrived in New York while the fighting continued but the winners were known. Loyalists were becoming more vulnerable and Britain still had a duty and obligation to them and a number of other minority groups.

Quakers generally practised pacifism in wars and the majority refused to take up arms on either side. This minority group was important to Digby and Britain since a large number of skilled Nantucket mariners and whalers had already moved to Nova Scotia and Britain. More would have been welcomed.

Pacifism in war calls for enormous courage. George Washington appeared ambivalent about the Quaker's refusal to bear arms against their fellow man. However, in May 1777, he wrote to Pennsylvania Governor W Livingston, "I have been informed…that the Quakers are disaffected and are doing all in their power to counteract your late Militia Law." Washington later commanded his officers to "take care that the unfriendly Quakers and others notoriously disaffected to the cause of American liberty, do not escape your Vigilance"[62].

In November 1775, Lord Dunmore, Royal Governor of Virginia, had issued a proclamation for all able bodied men to help the loyalist cause. "I do hereby declare all indented Servants, Negroes or others; free – that are able and willing to bear Arms, they joining His Majesty's Troops as soon as they may be…" The caveat was that the slaves belonged to rebel owners. Nevertheless, this was an historic emancipation proclamation.

The patriots subsequently reacted by offering freedom to the escaped slaves of loyalists and each side appeared to have some 4-5,000 black soldiers in both fighting and supporting roles. Nevertheless, the British later took their commitments to black recruits seriously.[63]

Another minority group was the United Empire Loyalists. This was an honorary title given to settlers in North America and elsewhere, who had asserted their loyalty to the Crown and

---

[61] Barnet Schecter, Battle for New York, p274
[62] EDSITEment Lesson 3
[63] BlackPast Org. Dunmore's Proclamation 1775

didn't support a complete break from Britain. A significant number of North American settlers didn't support the patriots and had already settled in Canada.

However, such groups as the Empire Loyalists in New York would be vulnerable once the city was re-occupied by the Continental government and would be faced with harsh treatment, robbery and even death. It was not uncommon to tar and feather individual loyalists, when the opportunity arose. This was another major problem for Admiral Digby and General Carleton to consider as the war was drawing to a close.

Kidnapping was a feature of this war on both sides. Captured senior officers could possibly be turned or used as hostages in exchange for their own officers who had been caught. Admiral Digby had partly based himself on land in Hanover Square in New York, while his ship the *Prince George* was fighting the French in the Caribbean, so he must have appeared a 'sitting duck'.

Prince William was also in Hanover Square, where he appeared to be popular with local citizens. These two high profile people were clearly exciting targets for kidnappers, so Colonel Mathius Ogden of the 1st New Jersey Continentals prepared a kidnapping plan. It would be a night raid using four whaleboats with muffled oars and sufficient handpicked soldiers to overcome an apparently light guard.

George Washington was enthusiastic and wrote, "The spirit and enterprise so conspicuous in your plan for surprising in their quarters, and bringing off, Prince William Henry and Admiral Digby merits applause, and you have my authority." Washington emphasised in a letter dated 28 March 1782 that there should be no "insult or indignity to the Persons of the Prince or Admiral" and Colonel Ogden should "impress the propriety of such conduct upon the party you command".[64]

In the end, Washington cancelled the operation when his spies in New York noticed that the British had increased the guards.

It really was war and peace. The fall of Yorktown in 1781 did not bring an immediate end to the war, partly because New York was still largely occupied by the British, but, nevertheless,

---

[64] Christian McBurney, Journal American Revolution / Digby

peace was in the air. Peace negotiations started in April 1782. The Treaty of Paris was signed on 3 September 1783 and was later ratified by the respective governments. Britain signed separate treaties with France and Spain.

The Treaty of Paris was clearly intended to be a genuine long-term peace treaty with phrases such as "forgetting all past misunderstandings & differences" and "securing to both perpetual peace and harmony". Both sides had distinguished, high calibre statesmen negotiating.

There are 10 well-known clauses but some were immediately material. Clauses 4, 5 and 6 largely focussed on recognising lawful contracted debts to be paid…on both sides. Clause 5 went further with Congress 'earnestly recommending' state legislatures to recognise rightful owners and providing restitution of all properties.

Clause 7 is interesting in that POWs on both sides would be released. The property of the British army (including slaves) now in the United States was to be forfeited. This proved contentious. General Cornwallis, who surrendered in Yorktown, couldn't stop his black troops from being enslaved again. Most British generals usually refused this command for their own black soldiers, since the curse of slavery was still rife.

Britain by this time had two outstanding military leaders in New York with General Carleton and Admiral Digby. Carleton improved the conditions of patriot prisoners on the prison ships and let most of them out on local islands in summer.

Following the surrender of New York, Admiral Digby allied with General Carleton to demand that Washington honour his promise to allow the United Empire Loyalists to leave the country "honourably and without molestation". The pair blatantly informed President Washington "that if his promises were not kept, they would resume hostilities without any further warning". They also stated that they would not wait for formal permission from London.[65]

Washington apparently took the commanders seriously since the British army was still a standing force. In spite of Yorktown, Britain still had tens of thousands of experienced soldiers in North America who could prolong the war for years.

---

[65] Digby's Naval Order Book. Admiral Digby Museum, Canada

Furthermore, Digby's naval blockade was biting into American trade and the merchants were restless.

Sir Guy Carleton claimed it would be a breach of honour and faith not to respect the British policy of freeing supporting slaves but if this policy conflicted with Clause 7 in the Treaty of Paris, then compensation would instead have to be paid to the appropriate slave owners.

Carleton initiated a register called the 'Book of Negroes' for taking names, ages, skills and names of former owners. Washington agreed, but there is some doubt whether these monies were ever paid, just as most loyalists probably never received compensation.

When it came to the navy escorting the loyalists from New York and elsewhere to the safe haven of Nova Scotia, Vice Admiral Digby took a personal hand. Peace was imminent, so Digby arranged for about 1500 loyalists to sail with him. Other loyalists and free slaves made the same journey before and after Digby. In all, more than 29,000 refugees left New York for Nova Scotia and St Johns in one year.[66]

Digby personally sailed in and commanded the *Atlanta* when his fleet arrived in Conway, a port in Nova Scotia, in early June 1783. Conway was renamed Digby in 1787 and is the location of the Admiral Digby Museum.

Digby was determined that the transportation would be successful. This determination can be seen by the iron in his commands in his Naval Order Book.

P 175. 17 April 1783. To Captain Mowat: "You are hereby required and directed to take HMS *Amphitrite* under your command, and whatever Transports or any other Vessels…under your Convoy… You are to proceed yourself…and to give them every Protection and assistance you can."

P 193. 9 July 1783. To Lieutenant Trounce: "You are hereby required and directed to receive on board His Majesty's Arm'd Storeship under your command all such Negroes as Captain Chads may send."[67]

Some of the freed people didn't settle well in the new colder climate and later chose to move to Sierra Leone, where the

---

[66] B Schecter, Battle for New York, p374
[67] Admiral Digby Museum, Canada

British had set up a new colony for the 'Black Poor' from London, which is another story.

Peace was in place on 28 November 1783 when the evacuation of New York was complete and Carleton left on 4 December, returning to Britain before embarking on new challenges at home and in Canada.

Digby stayed on. Signed treaties were yet to be ratified and this Admiral was prepared to stay, while there was still a single remaining loyalist who wanted to leave.

Digby had a lot on his mind returning to Britain in mid-1784. He had arrived in New York as a bachelor but was leaving with a wife. He had married an American widow called Eleanor Jauncey, who was now on board being taken for the first time, to his home near Winchester. Eleanor was yet to meet Digby's two sons, who were born out of wedlock. Since the son's unnamed mother was still around, the diplomacy would have been interesting.

During Digby's command on the American Station, he was not involved in major sea battles, but he imposed a very tight blockade which was having desperate effects on local merchants and the American economy.

Senator and financier Robert Morris had written a paper dated 10 May 1782 to John Hanson, President of Congress, about "The State of American commerce and the Plan of protecting it". The paper referred to 'Admiral R Digby' and stated "throughout the spring & summer of 1782, the blockade was overwhelmingly successful". He told Admiral de Grasse of France, "it is only by a kind of miracle that any vessel can get in or out."[68]

Digby had to consider another responsibility while sailing back to Britain, since he had been 'entrusted' by the Board of Longitude with Kendall's K2. Unlike Captain Phipps, he clearly wasn't 'hands on' in these matters. He didn't have the time while surviving in a war where a determined enemy, was forever plotting to kill or kidnap him.

Fortunately, he still had the faithful Robert Waddington on hand who was writing his report to Maskelyne and the Board of Longitude about K2 on this voyage. His report included:

---

[68] The Papers of Robert Morris, 1781–1784

"Having determined by a great number of observations – the Longitude of N. York, I set the Watch to Greenwich Mean Time & allowed such a rate of Gain as my experience – seemed to justify... We had made some Land whose Situation was ascertained by Lunar Observations (which have in no instance failed me) acquainted one with the Watch's Rate before we made any such land & so accurately, that I am confident we never erred a league in the Ships Place during a very long Passage to Antigua.

In April 1783 we sailed from the W. Indies for N. York – when allowing its extreme Gain of 16' on account of our advancing to the Northward, it gave the Longitude of the Lighthouse precisely. I feel the greatest confidence in asserting that this Time keeper aided only occasionally by Lunar Observations will determine the Place of a Ship with so much precision that if your Landfalls are ascertained in Position, there need not be a moment's apprehension for your Safety."

March 6, 1784, R Waddington[69]

Waddington, who had connections with the Board, had tested it thoroughly, proving K2 an important stepping stone towards widespread acceptance of marine chronometers.

Prior to Waddington's report, Digby had already returned K2 with a brief covering letter to the Board of Longitude when he referred the Board to the work of Waddington. He reported:

"Gentlemen. In general, he (Waddington) thinks it (K2) might be made more perfect, but in its present state, it may be of very great service at Sea in the hands of an attentive observer." R Digby, Jan 3, 1784

Digby retired from the sea in 1794 after promotion to full Admiral. His memories would surely have been of war and peace, love and marriage, sea blockades, diplomacy, royalty, young Nelson and witnessing the plight of loyal refugees and slaves.

---

[69] Waddington's report, 1784

Slaves. What was to become of the countless slaves? Meanwhile, K2 lay in Greenwich awaiting its next voyage, which was to Africa to explore an answer to that very question!

Chapter 7
Captain Thompson– West Coast Africa
1785 K2 4th Voyage

Edward Thompson was the third son of a business family and was born in November 1738. He had shown interest in the navy, so on becoming a teenager, he joined as a traditional midshipman on the *Stirling*, a 64-gun warship.[70]

Edward was bright and having passed his naval exams in November 1757 was subsequently promoted to lieutenant on the *Jason*. A move to the *Dorsetshire* under Captain Peter Denis brought him into the Seven Years War with blockade duties outside Brest and action at the Battle of Quiberon. In March 1760, Thompson moved to the *Bellona,* once again under his patron Peter Denis, until the end of the war when he was released on half pay.[71]

Edward Thompson had displayed his mariner enthusiasm and abilities in his naval exams and experience at sea, but he also had a second life, which was his love for the theatre and poetry. He proved his talents in the thespian world and was nicknamed 'Poet Thompson'. The freedom to follow his theatrical passion on land while on naval half-pay must have seemed a dream to him.

During this period, the poet in Thompson was especially active. A number of 'Meretricious Miscellanies' apparently penned by him were published in the book 'The Court of Cupid' in 1770, which was an anonymous collection of bawdy poems and satires. He may have thought that a low public profile would

---

[70] Whitehead 1785 to Ansty 1805
[71] "Edward Thompson" Laughton, John Knox, 1898

protect his naval career. Nevertheless, there were jealousies and one wag wrote of him:

> "Half a poet, half a tar,
> Half-fish, half-flesh,
> e'en what you will,
> Bred to the Bow-lines, not the Quill."[72]

Thompson had no personal fortune, so he later returned to sea on full pay with the hope of prize money. He had become a friend of the gregarious playwright, actor and producer David Garrick, who moved in wide social circles. Garrick may have had influential social connections in the Navy, having written the words for the song 'Heart of Oak' earlier in 1759. Thompson was not forgotten by the Navy in his other exciting world, since he was promoted to captain of the *Kingfisher* in 1771.

Peter Denis, Thompson's earlier captain on the *Bellona*, had by now been knighted and promoted to commander in chief of the Mediterranean fleet. Thompson subsequently got his own promotion to captain of the *Niger* in 1772 but with no current major wars, he was soon back in Britain again on half pay for nearly six years.

Thompson threw himself into his other life and revived an old play by Charles Shadwell for a production at Drury Lane in 1773, followed by 'The Syrens' played at Covent Garden. In 1775, he published 'The Case and Distressed Situation of the widows of the officers of the Navy'.

The call of the sea remained strong and in May 1778 Thompson was made captain of the *Hyaena*, a new 6th rate 24-gun frigate, carrying out convoy work to and from the West Indies.

By this time, Spain had entered the American Revolutionary war with the clear objective of taking back Gibraltar, strategically positioned in the gateway to the Mediterranean. A large British fleet under Sir George Rodney was gathering to lift the Spanish blockade and bring in supplies, so Thompson's new fast frigate was enlisted to help.

---

[72] Papers: Lady Ellinor Thompson

By coincidence, the *Prince George*, which was the Flagship of Admiral Digby in the American Station, had been released by Digby to assist in the relief of Gibraltar. K2 had been allocated to Digby, but with no ship, the timekeeper stayed behind on shore in New York with guardian Mr Waddington.

The first Battle of Cape St Vincent took place on 16 January 1780 and was hard fought between the fleets which carried on into the night, despite the Spanish being outgunned. It is sometimes called the 'Moonlight Battle'. It was a major victory for the Royal Navy at a crucial time in the European war.

In fairness to the Spanish admiral Don Juan de Langara, he sensibly tried to flee once he realised the size and strength of the British fleet but, in the chase, they were overtaken by the speed of the British ships using new copper-sheathed hulls.

Someone in a fast ship was needed to take the good news back to Britain. The Admiralty Office confirmed on 28 Feb 1780 that "Captain Edward Thompson of His Majesty's ship *Hyaena* arrived early this morning from Gibraltar with dispatches from Admiral Sir George Rodney"[73]. The dispatch dated 27 January 1780, Gibraltar Bay, stated:

"Sir, it is with the highest satisfaction, I can congratulate their lordships on a signal victory obtained by His Majesty's ships under my command, over the Spanish squadron commanded by Don Juan Langara, wherein the greatest part of this squadron were either taken or destroyed..."

Thompson, no doubt, bathed in the glory of bringing such good news, but he was rapidly sent back to the New World. He spent two years in convoy work and governance of Caribbean colonies where he was exposed to the global business of slavery. Thompson believed the Americans were his brothers, until the French joined the war.

In 1783, Thompson was appointed to the *Grampus*, a 50-gunner due to sail to West Africa in a small squadron, of which he would be overall commodore.[74]

---

[73] London Gazette Extraordinary
[74] AIM25 collection, ref 0064 THM

Commodore Thompson received his *Grampus* captaincy commission on 19 July 1783 which was headed "By the Commissioners for Executing the Office of Lord High Admiral of Great Britain and Ireland And of all His Majesty's Plantations... We do hereby constitute and appoint you as Captain of His Majesty's ship the Grampus. Requiring you forthwith to go on board for the Charge and Command"[75].

Thompson was persuaded by Lord Sydney to delay the main voyage because of the uncertainty of the effects of the war on America where convicts used to be conveniently sent. It was decided that Thompson should carry out a reconnaissance of the coastal areas of northwest Africa in the *Grampus* to ascertain the possibility of new convict settlements.

Thompson left England in mid-1783 focusing on Gambia and acquainting himself with the disasters and the evacuation of Fort Mori following a murder and convict soldiers running amok. He was disappointed with the habitable options for both British convicts and the freed slaves from the American war.

The 'Botany Bay Decision' was made to create a penal colony in New South Wales, Australia as it was deemed to be healthier for European convicts.

The subsequent main expedition to the coast of West Africa in 1785 consisted of two ships and was described as a "voyage of discovery".

The year running up to mid-1785 was a frustrating time for Thompson, since the *Grampus* was moored at either Spithead or Portsmouth harbour for repairs. There were meetings with the great and the good, but he may have also spent time in his thespian world. The latter part of the Captain's Journal while on shore, was delegated to 1st Lieutenant Alexander Kirkwood, who signed off the Journal for the Admiralty on 28 July 1785.[76]

This temporary delegation in command gave Thompson an opportunity to exchange his sword for his writer's pen. A verse from his satire 'The Wiltshire Beau':

---

[75] Admiralty Commission, NMM

[76] Grampus Log

"Would ye, ye Fair, be cautious whom ye prove, Ye rarely meet a true return in Love, The Man of Courage, and the Man of Sense, Never betray the lovely innocence; By Heav'n they're sent to save and guard the Fair; And make your Virtue their peculiar care; The fool alone disturbs your bless'd repose, The Men of Sense were never Virtue's foes."[77]

July 1785 was also the time that Lieutenant Home Riggs Popham arrived at Spithead proudly clutching an instrument personally entrusted to him by the Board of Longitude. He claimed "It was for determining the longitude by a watch made by Mr Kendall on his own construction". He had met up with Mr Kendall who gave K2 "into my charge".

Popham had volunteered for this voyage since he had sailed with Captain Thompson on the frigate *Hyaena* and who was his mentor. Popham had since been promoted and was a 'marine surveyor'.

At last, they were ready for sea on the 28 July, but delayed for the next two days. They also had to liaise with the sloop *Nautilus* which was joining them.[78]

This small squadron was sailing under 'private orders'; once at sea, all would be revealed. It had been organised and largely financed by the 'Committee for the Relief of Black Poor' supported by slave abolitionists, wealthy individuals, philanthropists and political figures such as Wilberforce. The objective was to find a new home in Africa for slaves where they could live as free people. The purpose of the expedition was to survey the coast of West and South West Africa, seeking suitable locations for such a settlement and colony.

The British government provided two warships to give teeth to this small fleet. There was a Polish botanist on board with such an unpronounceable name that he was referred to as 'Hove'. He would be vital when seeking habitable land.

One reason for Thompson being commodore of the expedition might have been his reputation for "his commiseration of suffering and injustice…he never lost an opportunity to wield his pen to try to right what in his view was

---

[77] The Meretriciad. Anonymous, Edward Thompson
[78] Grampus Log, 28/30.07.1785

81

wrong". Earlier at sea, in 1781, he wrote 'An African Tale' about a ship called *Fanny*. Two verses:

> *"From Liverpool a gallant ship,*
> *With tackle trim and gay,*
> *Sail'd with a very wicked freight,*
> *For Slaves of Africa.*
>
> *Nor are the Merchants callous souls,*
> *Less Piteous than the Knaves,*
> *Which they employ on Guinea Coast,*
> *To buy, or steal the slaves."*[79]

It made sense that the smaller sloop *Nautilus* would be more suitable to venture up creeks and make landings while the larger 50-gun *Grampus* would provide strength and show the flag to other European powers.

The log book clearly showed which navigational instruments to identify longitude were being used on any particular day, identified by a code under headings

Dead Reckoning (DR) and Sextant (S) were generally shown under the Latitude column as well as Longitude. 'Remarks' were on the opposite page, as a journal. There did not appear to be any debate or comment comparing these navigational techniques, of which two methods were generally used. However, whenever only one method was recorded, Time Piece (TP) appears more often than Lunar (L). This could indicate that the officers responsible for navigation gradually became confident with K2.

On October 1, they passed Finisterre, a rocky peninsula off Galicia on the West of Spain. When sighting Oporto in Portugal on 5 October, signals were exchanged.

The *Grampus* moored in Funchal Bay in Madera, on Saturday 8 October and the Longitudes logged were:

S=11.45 **TP**=11.58 **L**=11.35.

Probably, an average figure would be taken.

---

[79] Papers: Lady Ellinor Thompson

The *Grampus* stayed in Madeira until the 24 October. The Royal Navy had important priorities, so apart from fresh food, vast quantities of Portuguese Madeira wine would be loaded. This preserved well on voyages, being fortified with neutral grape spirit.

On 25 and 26 October, the crew could see the peak of Tenerife, the largest island in the Canaries, and Cape Verde on 9 November. They then entered West African waters a few hundred miles off Dakar in Senegal.

They headed towards Goree Island just 3 kilometres from Dakar. It was a trading post for the Atlantic slave trade and was called the 'House of Slaves' featuring 'The Door of No Return'. Initially a Portuguese post, it changed hands repeatedly between Britain, Holland and France.

When mooring in Goree Bay on 10 November, soundings were taken and an eleven gun salute was returned by the fort. The small fleet of the *Grampus* and *Nautilus*, moved on after four days. The *Grampus* journal doesn't often mention the *Nautilus*, possibly indicating that the sloop was often on its own, closer to shore.

Based on the Captain's log, after 27 November, the *Grampus* navigators appeared to rely almost exclusively on K2 for finding Longitude off West Africa. This seems a success for K2 and chronometer technology.[80]

However, Lieutenant Popham was writing his own journal on K2 for the Board of Longitude. This was a personal assignment for Popham, who was keeping a completely separate document to the Captain's journal. Thompson appeared interested in comparing different navigational instruments and methods. Popham, however, appeared to focus on using the Time Piece, to identify the position of locations visited. He described his last conversation with Larcum Kendall:

"The watch was 3'11" too fast for Mean Time and 1'11" too slow for Greenwich Time and 49" too slow for London Time. He told me he found it was losing time, he had raised the spring and had no doubt that I should find it was gaining when I had an

---

[80] Grampus Log Book

opportunity of timing its rate." Subsequently, Popham, with greater understanding, was able to make reasonable position allowances.[81]

On 11 December, the *Grampus* and *Nautilus* moored at Cape Apollonia, on the 'Gold Coast'. Built by the British in 1691 to keep out the Dutch, it inevitably played a part in the slave trade. It became uneconomic by 1819 once the slave trade was abolished.

The coast of West Africa was littered with forts, many of which would become obsolete. Thompson in December and January would either pass by them or stop for a short time. One of the biggest forts was Accra in Ghana where they moored about six miles from the fort on 12 January 1786, firing morning and evening gun salutes. On 13 January, Captain Thompson repeated the firing of morning and evening guns. Also, in his Journal that day, he included a single word: "Sick."

On 17 January 1786, the *Grampus* received two tons of water from the *Nautilus*, which was tendering for the flagship.

On the same day, Lieutenant Alexander Kirkwood recorded: "On this day at 14 past 4, departed this life of Commander Edward Thompson upon which the command devolved to George Tripp Esq, Commander of HM Sloop *Nautilus*. At 8 shortened sails."

The earlier log entries on both 16 and 17 January appear to be in the handwriting of Lieutenant Kirkwood, which indicates Captain Thompson had been fading rapidly. This coast was later aptly called 'White Man's Grave'. Captain Tripp became responsible for completing the *Grampus* voyage and returning to England.

Ironically, the 19 years old Lieutenant Thomas Boulden Thompson on the *Grampus* took over the captaincy of the *Nautilus* from Captain Tripp. He was a nephew of Edward Thompson and had been brought up by him as his own son and heir. The nephew added the surname 'Thompson' after his birth surname, Boulden.

---

[81] Board of Longitude Collections RGO 14/51

Commodore Edward Thompson, nicknamed 'Ned', had taken the education of Thomas so seriously that many whispered he was the youth's blood father. Thomas had even sailed under his uncle on the *Hyaena* at the Battle of St Vincent. Just after the death, Thomas said he had lost "my only friend and parent"[82]. He was not alone, "this ship was filled with lamentation". Popham, like Thomas, had sailed on the *Hyaena* and also regarded Commodore Edward Thompson as a father figure.

Being in the tropics, Captain Thompson was rapidly buried at sea the following day with musket and cannon fire. It was later revealed that his dream had been to be the first governor of the new settlement.

There is a belief that Edward Thompson was unmarried. That is not quite true; indeed, it's a myth. In the second line of his will, it states: "To Mary Thompson my ungrateful wife, I bequeath One Hundred Pounds." Even today one can taste the bitterness in that single line. Kirkwood was left a gold cane and some silver buckles. Young Thomas Boulden Thompson got the lion's share.

It may be a fitting remembrance of him and his dark humour to finish with his own epitaph:

"Ned Thompson at last is sail'd out of this world,
His shrouds are cast off, and his top sails are furled,
He lies snug in death's boat, without any concern,
And is moor'd for a full due a-head and a-stern,
O'er the compass of his life he has merrily run
His reck'ning is out, and his voyage, it is done!"[83]

Thomas took over responsibility for the *Nautilus's* part of the voyage two weeks later and continued the journey of discovery, surveying West and South West Africa looking for suitable locations for settlements for both convicts and freed slaves. He was accompanied by Lieutenant Popham since it had already been planned that this 'marine surveyor' would transfer to the *Nautilus* when the ships parted company and he would take K2 with him on this more dangerous voyage.

---

[82] A Merciless Place, Emma Thompson, p321/3
[83] Papers: Lady Ellinor Thompson

Thomas Thompson loaded supplies from the *Grampus* to the *Nautilus* which headed South on what turned out to be an exhausting and disappointing expedition. They surveyed the South West coast reaching about 100 miles North of Cape Town without finding "a drop of water or a tree". It was joked, "The only plant growing here is a small Geranium."

Before returning to England in July 1786 Thomas must have concluded that Sierra Leone was the best option. This was debated back in England where the First Fleet to Australia was being planned. There appeared to be some consensus that West Africa was suitable for free slaves but the climate wouldn't suit most white prisoners.

Captain Trigg headed straight back to England in the *Grampus*, after leaving the *Nautilus* on 2 February. He received his new Admiralty Commission as 'Commander of the *Grampus* on 27 March 1786. Although still at sea, the commission for Captain Thomas Bolden Thompson was also issued on the same day for 'Captain of *Nautilus*'.

Popham continued to use K2 on the *Nautilus* taking positions of every place they visited. He had signed for K2 in 1785 and was charged with responsibilities which appeared to include personally returning it. He returned K2 on 23 July 1786 with his journal to the Board of Longitude. A receipt was given dated 10 August 1786.[84]

Whereas the *Grampus* log contained the letter for each navigational tool, Popham's own report appeared to have only had one column 'Time W', presumably for 'Time Watch'.

Popham had a distinguished naval career in battle as well as in designing a new signalling system before becoming a Rear Admiral. He was also knighted and became an MP. His colourful life fluctuated between wealth and poverty.

Captain Thomas Boulden Thompson subsequently led three transports in the *Nautilus* back to the Sierra Leone River to establish a free colony for nearly 400 'Black Poor', combined with some white artisans and prostitutes. Thomas bought land "for-ever" from a local chief called King Tom but it was not viable without professional military support.[85] The colony was

---

[84] Cambridge RGO 14/9

[85] British Empire, R Gott, 91/2

called 'The Province of Freedom' but rapidly dropped in numbers due to disease, local contention and slavers.

In March 1792, 1192 ex slaves who had fled to Nova Scotia from America also landed in this new colony. They had boarded in Halifax, many having been tempted by promises of 20 acres of land and the numbers started to make the settlement more credible.[86] However, all these initial attempts appeared to end in different degrees of disaster, made worse by a French attack on the small colony.

Freetown was managed by the Sierra Leone Company which was later financed by well-meaning supporters and investors. It took many years for Sierra Leone to become a working colony. The Royal Navy made 'Freetown' their base in 1808 for the West African Station.

Up to this 4th voyage, K2 had seemed to be a lucky charm. The ship that took it to the Arctic would have been crushed by ice and perhaps all souls would have been lost but for a timely wind change. The two later ships operating in North America at different times, survived fire and powder ships, gunfire, a submarine, floating mines and kidnapping plots. K2 survived the African equatorial climate on this voyage, but its luck ran out with the death of the Commander.

However, already another naval captain who had experience of K1 and K3 sailing with Cook in the Pacific was being offered K2 by the Admiralty. The next voyage would just involve sailing to a beautiful South Pacific island where the officers only had to rub noses with some nice Polynesian chiefs and the crew only had to behave. It just involved digging up a few plants and transporting them to another beautiful island – in the Caribbean. Easy. Surely, nothing could go wrong?

---

[86] Black Loyalists Search for Promised Land. James St G Walker

Chapter 8
Captain Bligh – Bounty-South Pacific
1787 K2 5th Voyage

By 1787, the talented 33-year-old Lieutenant William Bligh RN had some powerful friends. He valued such friends and was careful to acknowledge their contributions to the immediate *Bounty* expedition.

He started his later written account of the *Bounty* expedition: "The King having been graciously pleased to comply with a request from the merchants and planters interested in his Majesty's West India possessions, that the bread-fruit tree might be introduced into these islands, a vessel, proper for the undertaking, was bought, and taken dock at Deptford, to be provided with the necessary fixtures and preparations for executing the objective of the voyage. These were completed according to a plan of my much honoured friend, Sir Joseph Banks."[87]

Bligh had previously sailed as the ship's master on the *Resolution* on Captain Cook's 3rd and fatal voyage. His navigational talents had been noted and were particularly useful after Cook's death on the beaches of Hawaii in 1779. In December 1777, Cook had appeared to honour him by naming a small high rock 'Bligh Cape' on misty islands off British Columbia that he thought could be the isle of Rendezvous. Cook later dryly commented: "I know nothing that can Rendezvous at it, but the fowls of the air."[88]

It all might have been different if Cook had survived this 3rd expedition. Bligh left the *Resolution* in 1780, unhappy that he

---

[87] Ch.1, Captains Bligh's Account
[88] Cook's Journal, p441/2

and his ability hadn't been really appreciated. Two other lieutenants had been promoted to Post Captains after the voyage finished and he had not. He appeared to particularly resent First Lieutenant James King who took over as Captain. Bligh's temper, both verbal and written, showed up more towards the end of this voyage when he began to perceive James as undeserving, ignoring the fact that King was both polished and able. Bligh had largely worked his way up by his talents and believed others enjoyed privilege and patronage.[89]

Possibly, Bligh could see in men such as James King and even Fletcher Christian, how accepted they were in society and how comfortable they were amongst the ranks of gentlemen. Jealousy can be intensely corrosive; Oxford Dict. "vindictive through envy". Were the seeds of darkness in Bligh's character already being planted – ready to burst out on his next long voyage?

In between the two long South Seas voyages, Bligh re-visited the Isle of Man where he met up with the Betham family, leading to his marriage to their daughter, Elizabeth, who was fiercely loyal to the end. Her uncle Duncan Campbell took on Bligh to command some of his merchant ships trading to and from the West Indies. This was temporary employment but Bligh now had his own connections with maritime contacts…

Bligh continued, "The ship was named the *Bounty* and I was appointed to command her on 16 August 1787. Her burden was nearly 215 tons; her extreme length on deck, 90 feet 10 inches; extreme breadth 24 feet 3 inches; and height in the hold under the beams, at the main hatchway, 10 feet three inches."

Bligh displayed real sea going experience by having the masts shortened and reducing the ballast since it could be 'too much dead weight in their bottom'.

Resolution (461 tonnes); *Discovery* (298 tonnes), *Endeavour* (368 tonnes) and *Adventure* (340 tonnes) were all current exploration ships. Although the *Bounty* (215 tonnes) had a smaller compliment, the crew and officers would be living much closer together, 'cheek by jowl'.

---

[89] P Haughton, Fatal Voyage, p23, and S Ragnall, Better Conceived, p45

These were mainly Whitby Colliers which were sturdy, relatively cheap, had ample holding space, needed minimum crew and were blessed with a reasonably shallow draft for marine exploration. They were primarily made in Whitby and Scarborough in NE England, for carrying commercial coastal coal, tendering the Navy and were ideal for Bligh's *Bounty*.

When Cook had years earlier considered the *Endeavour*, the name had already been changed from the *Drake* to avoid upsetting the Spanish in the Pacific, who still regarded the English hero as a pirate. Cook said, "A better ship for such purposes I could never wish for." He must have been grateful for its strength when stuck on the Australian Barrier Reef.

In the case of the *Bounty*, the ship had already been chosen by Banks at the minimum level of suitability, limited by a lack of commitment by the Admiralty. It was 'sloop' rated which meant it could be commanded by a junior lieutenant without a contingent of marines. Bligh had no way of changing the situation but promoted Christian to 'acting lieutenant'.

The full establishment of men and officers for the ship totalled 46. Bligh must have been pleased to be joined by some previously known sailors and personnel. "Two skilful and careful men were appointed, at Sir Joseph Bank's recommendation, to have management of the plants... the one David Nelson, who had been on similar employment in Captain Cook's last voyage; the other William Brown, previously Nelson's assistant."

Another familiar face was William Peckover, a gunner who sailed with Cook on three voyages, two as a gunner and now as an able bodied seaman already ranking a warrant officer on the *Endeavour*. He had a good knowledge of the Tahitian language and was clearly a highly valuable member of the crew. David Nelson and Peckover would later share the launch with Lieutenant Bligh on their trip to Timor.

Looking for other crew members he could count on for support, Bligh invited Fletcher Christian to join the *Bounty* voyage. Christian had worked as an apprentice under his command on the *Britannia*, while waiting for an officer's position and he also had connections which might be useful.

Bligh gave Fletcher a chance. Fletcher, ten years younger, believed he could handle Bligh![90]

"The ship was stored and victualled for 18 months," said Bligh, who was incredibly health conscious and insisted on extra quantities of sauerkraut and malt to fend off scurvy. "I was likewise furnished with a quantity of iron-work and trinkets, to serve in our intercourse with the natives in the South Seas and from the Board of Longitude I received a timekeeper, made by Mr. Kendall."[91] Bligh had experience of K1 as master on the *Resolution* with Cook on his 3rd voyage and also with K3 on the supporting ship *Discovery*, so he must have been overjoyed to be allocated K2 for the *Bounty*. A receipt for this precious instrument was duly signed.

On 15 October 1787, Bligh received orders to proceed to Spithead with K2 where "the rate of the timepiece was several times examined by Mr. Bailey's observations at the Portsmouth observatory. On 19 December, the last time of it being examined on shore, it was 1' 52",5 too fast for mean time, and then losing at the rate of 1' 1" per day and at this rate I estimate its going when we sailed".

The written orders Bligh received from the office of the Lord High Admiral were very specific and included: "You are in pursuance of his Majesty's pleasure, signified to us by Lord Sydney, one of the principal secretaries of state, hereby required and directed to put to seas in the vessel you command, the first favourable opportunity of wind and weather, and proceed with her, as expeditiously as possible 'round Cape Horn, to the Society Islands, situated in the Southern ocean, in the latitude of about 18° S, and longitude of about 210° E, from Greenwich, where, according to the late Captain Cook and persons…the bread-fruit tree is to be found in the most luxuriant state."

These were amended to give Bligh some flexibility: "The year being now so far advanced, it is probable…you will be too late for your passing 'round Cape Horn without much difficulty and hazard; you are, in that case at liberty…to proceed in her to Otaheite, 'round the Cape of Good Hope."

---

[90] RD Madision, Captain Bligh's Account
[91] Ch.2–5, Captain Bligh's Account

Given under our hands, 18 December 1787
Howe

The departure was "Sunday, 23 December 1787, we sailed from Spithead and passing through the Needles, directed our course down channel".

The first port of call was Tenerife and Bligh, noting two rocks at the northern boundary, chose to make an observation at noon, giving the latitude 28° 44'N and their longitude by our timekeeper 16° 5'W. Bligh had seized the opportunity to use K2.

Once anchored, Bligh sent Christian ashore to contact the governor and request permission to land, make some repairs and purchase further victuals. Christian was also to declare that the *Bounty* would salute, provided an equal number of guns responded. The reply was courteous but declined a returning gun salute since the governor could only do so "to persons equal in rank to himself". Bligh must have felt piqued by this diplomatic snub.

During the visit, weather prevented taking lunar observations to help find longitude, but with the K2-timekeeper: "I have computed the situation of the town of Santa Cruz to be 28° 28' N latitude, and 16° 18' W longitude." Bligh also noted that a reading from his compass was five degrees different to one he had taken eleven years earlier. He pondered on the uncertainties of variations of the magnetic pole, concluding comparisons should use the same compass at exactly the same spot.

The *Bounty* left Tenerife 10 January 1788 with "the ship's company all in good health and spirits". Bligh quickly introduced the three-watch system instead of two, in order to allow unbroken sleep for the "health of the ship's company". He also directed drinking water "to be filtered through dripstones, bought at Tenerife". The *Bounty* continued on an SSW direction towards the South Atlantic.

On Monday, 4 Feb, "Had very heavy rain; during which we nearly filled our empty casks of water. So much wet weather, with the closeness of the air, covered everything with mildew. The ship was aired below with fires and frequently sprinkled with vinegar." Part of Bligh's health regime included daily dancing to Byrne, the blind fiddler who had been invited on board by Bligh to exercise the crew, weather permitting.

Monday 18 Feb, "In the course of this day's run, the variation changed from West to East. Great attention paid to keeping clean and wholesome. Giving all air possible to drying and airing people's clothes and bedding". A few days later, "we caught a shark and five dolphins… Four days tried for soundings and finding no bottom."

Sunday 2 March, "I gave to Fletcher Christian, whom I had before directed to take charge of the 3rd watch, a written order to act a lieutenant. Bligh gave Mathew Quintal two dozen lashes for 'insolence and mutinous behaviour'! Quintal never forgot or forgave this savage punishment and subsequently, became one of the key mutineers."

19 March, "At noon by my account, we were within twenty leagues of Port Desire. N W winds with thick foggy weather." Four days later, "nine in the forenoon we were off Cape St Diego, the eastern part of Terra del Fuego". Bligh was at his best, "gladly agreeing to the men's request for straight grog instead of watered down, to keep out the cold".[92]

4 April, there were flocks of albatrosses, small blue petrels and pintada, some of which were caught. The method was to fasten the bait a foot or two before the hook and "by giving the line a sudden jerk when the bird was at the bait, it was hooked in the feet or body". The albatross was the best catch and could be fattened up for a few days on corn. Was this albatross possibly a dark omen?

> *Ah! Well a day! What evil looks*
> *Had I from old and young!*
> *Instead of the cross, the Albatross*
> *About my neck was hung.*

> Coleridge.

Bligh would have done well to be more wary of killing albatrosses with bad luck lurking around the corner. Just 10 years later, Coleridge's Ancient Mariner was cursed as punishment, for doing just that.

---

[92] R Hough, The Bounty, p72

10 April, "The stormy weather continued with a great sea." Bligh was desperate to change course from trying to go west around South America instead of going east past South Africa. He wrote,

"The prevalence of the westerly winds in high latitudes, left me no reason to doubt of making a quick passage to the Cape of Good Hope, and thence to the eastward 'round New Holland."

On 22 April, "I ordered the helm to be to be put to weather, to the joy of every person on board". After turning towards Africa, Bligh commended the crew, "You have endured much and I congratulate and thank you all" to a burst of cheers.

How many mariners heading to the tip of South Africa with the help of the westerlies, must have thought that 'The Cape of Good Hope' was such a great name? Thursday 22 May 1788 "we saw the Table Mountain".

"As it is reckoned unsafe riding in Table Bay at this time of the year, I steered for False Bay." The *Bounty* was then secured in an area called Simon's Bay. Bligh saluted the fort and must have been relieved that it was returned with an equal number of guns. Bligh went ashore to meet the governor and give directions for supplies and repairs.

The *Bounty* was leaking and needed caulking. They also set about repairing sails and rigging and checking existing stores. "The timekeeper I took on shore to ascertain its rate, and other instruments, to make astronomical observations." The physical effort of attempting to round Cape Horn in storms must have been a challenging 'sea going test' for K2.

On 29 June, being ready for sea, "I took the timekeeper and instruments on board. The error on the time keeper was 3' 33", too slow for the mean time at Greenwich, and its rate of going 3" per day losing. We sailed at four o' clock this afternoon, and saluted the platform with thirteen guns as we ran out of the bay, which was again returned".

Leaving the Cape of Good Hope after 38 days on 1 July, for Van Diemen's Land (Tasmania) the winds were "mostly from the westward, very boisterous but…in this season…free from fogs". Because of the westerly current, "the ship was every day westward of the reckoning, because of drift". This stretch of sailing was the longest part of the voyage; some 6,000 miles in 23 days, thanks largely to Bligh's navigation.

Tasmania was not yet known to be an island and still regarded as a physical part of Australia, which is why they steered south of all land. Sighting the coast of Tasmania on 19 August, Bligh moved into Adventure Bay for anchorage and landing. "The ship being moored, I went in a boat to look…for wood and water." Having been there with Cook in January 1777, he found no signs of other European or native visits.

The tasks of wooding and watering continued. They then saw on the trunk of a dead tree the initials "A.D. 1773" carved. They speculated that it was possibly from Captain Furneaux's voyage? Mr Nelson planted some fruit trees from South Africa to benefit future voyagers.

They were ready to start the last leg of the voyage to Tahiti on 4 September 1788. Bligh and the *Bounty* proceeded to 'island and bay hop' for nearly two months intending to pass to the southward of New Zealand. "On 14 September, we were in 49° 24 S latitude and in 168° 3' E longitude, which is on the same meridian with the south end of New Zealand. I have named some islands after the ship, the *Bounty* Isles."

They passed Meitei on 25 October 1788 latitude 17° 53' S, and by the K2-timekeeper, its longitude was 18 24' E from Point Venus and later in the evening could see Otaheite. "On the 26th, we anchored in Matavai Bay in 13 fathoms." Excitement mounted. Considering the amount of time likely to be spent on this island and lack of 'reserve' of sailors, Bligh noted:

"I ordered every person to be examined by the surgeon, and had the satisfaction to learn from his report they were all perfectly free from any venereal complaint." Everyone should have been happy in this paradise, but it was not the case. The surgeon was incompetent and soon died from alcoholism.

Chapter 9
The Mutiny – The Fate of K2
1789

The *Bounty* had reached its destination. Otaheite. Paradise. There did not appear to be any spectres or omens of disaster. Although much has been written about this nugget of history, the drama of this conflict also plays a pivotal part in this story of the K2 Bounty Watch.

Several chiefs came on board to welcome the travellers and appeared delighted to see Lieutenant Bligh again, remembering him from Captain Cook's days. Bligh noted: "As soon as the ship was secured, I went on shore with the chief Poeeno, accompanied by a multitude of the natives. He conducted me to the place where we had fixed our tents in 1777 and desired that I would now appropriate the spot to the same use."[93]

As expected, there was much mutual entertainment and exchange of presents. Peckover, the gunner, was charged with the responsibility of managing this traffic with the island natives since he was quite fluent in their language. The chiefs showed their pleasure in Western products and Bligh was generous with his gifts, to assist his objective of collecting young bread fruit trees.

Bligh sent the gardener Nelson and his assistant Brown to look for these plants and took pleasure in their report "that my mission would probably be accomplished with ease". The officers and crew had been instructed not to mention the objective "lest it might enhance the value of the bread fruit plants". All was well.

---

[93] Bligh's Narrative, p40

An islander brought a painting of Captain Cook which had been done by Webber in 1777 for ruling chief, Tinah (also called Otoo) to have the broken frame repaired. The Polynesians counted time in moons, so they declared that Cook had left them 63 moons ago. Their Cook picture was always displayed to visiting English ships to show friendship. The chiefs were disappointed that the *Bounty* had not brought another artist.

Relationships blossomed rapidly and Bligh commented: "an intimacy between the natives and our people, was already so general, that there was scarce a man in the ship who had not his 'tyo' or friend"[94]. Over time, this included genuine romantic relationships that ultimately produced a new generation and unwittingly, encouraged British sailors to defy authority. Sex is a powerful driving force for all mammals.

Bligh noticed that the bread fruit trees appeared to be full of fruit and played his commercial role carefully; so when visiting a particular district of Matavai called Oparre, he mentioned to chief Tinah that he was going to visit other islands as well to fulfil the wishes of King George. Tinah did not like that, saying there was no need to leave Matavai. "Here", said he, "you shall be supplied plentifully with everything you want. All here are your friends and friends of King George." Bligh finally revealed that King George desired bread fruit trees and Chief Tinah promised that a great number would be put on board, pleased that he could satisfy the King so easily.

An area was set aside with the consent of Tinah and other chiefs, which would be exclusively used for collecting the young bread-fruit plants. Tents were erected and managed by a party of nine people under the head gardener Mr Nelson. This facility also meant that the natives could easily bring such plants to this spot instead of to the ship. Meanwhile, the cycle of entertaining continued, which was a tribute to Bligh's social stamina.

In February 1789, three of the *Bounty's* sailors including Churchill, the ship's corporal, accompanied by seamen Musprat and Millward, deserted the ship taking the cutter and some arms. Bligh received information that the deserters had also taken a

---

[94] Ibid, p42

native sailing boat and were heading for another island. Some locals returned the *Bounty's* cutter and were lavishly rewarded. They then enthusiastically offered to also capture the culprits.[95]

After another week, Bligh received information that the deserters were 5 miles away, so he prepared the cutter with various Tahitians joining in. Bligh carried out a night raid and when challenged in a house, the deserters came out surrendering, with their arms in the air. They claimed they would have returned earlier but for the Polynesians trying to catch them.

Desertion was a very serious offence in the Royal Navy and could lead to savage flogging or even hanging. Bligh was no doubt considering punishments but appeared completely oblivious of the background and implications of the desertions. Was morale low? Was discipline eroding? Was this a warning of things to come? Bligh reported that he flogged Isaac Martin with 19 lashes for striking a native. However, Bligh didn't seem to mention of the punishment for these three deserters in his written 'account'.

A later report by James Morrison in his 'Sailor's Account' clearly stated that these three deserters were immediately put in irons and flogged a month later. Churchill received two dozen lashes while Musprat and Millard each received four dozen lashes and were immediately put back to work. That appears more credible. Bligh would later discover that not surprisingly, all three of these deserters and Martin subsequently sided with the mutineers.

Bligh was anxious about the K2 marine timekeeper. Having been away that night and weather preventing a return to the ship, he reported that the timekeeper went down at 10h 5' 36". "I set it going again by a common watch, corrected by observations, and endeavoured to make the error the same as if it had not stopped."[96]

On 27 February, Bligh claimed that "the plants are in a very fine state and Mr Nelson thinks they will be perfectly established in the pots in the course of a month"[97]. Bligh highly valued his gardener not only to look after the plants, but also as a friend.

---

[95] Ibid, p70

[96] Ibid, p74

[97] R Hough, The Bounty, p108

Monday, 2 March, Mr Peckover had some bedding stolen with a water cask and part of an azimuth compass. Chief Tinah arranged for the return of the water cask and the compass part, leaving Bligh to persuade the captured villain to return the bedding. The thief was not a local so received a severe flogging. Peckover was also tasked to limit the crew's souvenirs to just their own sea trunks, since the ship was full enough already.

Friday, 3 April 1789, there was much coming and going the day before departure. More presents were exchanged and the repaired picture of Captain Cook was returned to Tinah. Daylight on Saturday 4th, the *Bounty* unmoored and slowly made out to sea. Tinah received a promised pair of pistols and there was a lot of mutual cheering on leaving Otaheite after twenty three weeks. A native parting was: *"May the Eatua (God) protect you, forever and ever."*

Most of the mariners were ready to go. There appeared to be only three serious relationships with Polynesian women. These were Christian, Alex Smith and Quintal, all of whom had stayed loyal to their one partner for the whole stay. Interestingly, all three were key mutineers.

The *Bounty* had three weeks sailing from Tahiti in the Society Islands to Tofoa in the Friendly Islands. The relationship between Bligh and Christian continued to deteriorate. The long stay away from the ship in Tahiti had eroded discipline and Bligh's capacity to criticise any minor failure of duty was having a malign effect.

In fairness to Bligh, his acting lieutenant Christian turning up adorned with Polynesian love tattoos on his body might have added fuel to the fire. Bligh did also have issues with Fryer and Purcell but one witness commented: "Whatever fault was found, Mr. Christian was sure to bear the brunt of the captain's anger." In the subsequent trials and proceedings, it seems difficult to find a bad word spoken against Christian from the *Bounty* crew.

While on shore filling casks with water at Annamooka, Christian and others were continuously taunted and threatened by natives. Being under orders not to fire, he reported to Bligh: "I am having great difficulty carrying out my duties, sir."

Bligh retorted: "You damned cowardly rascal."[98] The arguments became more frequent.

Christian's despair became palpable. Some of the officers and crew kept their coconuts on deck. Christian was openly accused by Bligh's of taking some of his coconuts to eat, while on his watch. A denial led to "you lie, you scoundrel. You have taken one half". Bligh continued, "you damned hound. You must have stolen half of them or you could give a better account." This retort was delivered with Bligh's fist in Christian's face. This incident lasted some time as Bligh hysterically challenged everyone in sight. Finally, he calmed down saying, "The people may take their nuts below."

Purcell, a warrant officer, was sympathetic to Christian whose despair was deepening: "I would rather die ten thousand deaths than bear this treatment any longer."[99] Bligh had the ability to quickly change his manner and moods. Bligh's apparent madness, suspicions, abusive language, changing moods and temper were all boiling in a tight confined space.

7.30 pm, 27 April 1789, Bligh's servant sent a message to the depressed Christian inviting him to supper. This had happened in the past after a conflict, and he replied to the servant, "Tell Mr Bligh that I am indisposed, Jack, and give him my compliments." Perhaps madness is catching since Christian had already built a small raft and set aside provisions to try his luck as a deserter on local islands. Mr Stewart relieved the night watch and finding the raft persuaded him to drop the idea, saying, "The people are ripe for anything." There was now another option.[100]

Awake bold Bligh! The foe is at the gate!
Awake! Awake!-Alas it is too late!
Fiercely beside thy cot the mutineer
Stands, and proclaims the reign of rage and fear,
Thy limbs are bound, the bayonet at thy breast,
The hands, which trembled at the voice, arrest,
Dragged o'er the deck, no more at thy command.

Lord Byron

---

[98] Ibid, p119
[99] Ibid, p179
[100] James Morrison, Sailor's Account, p39

5.30 am, Tuesday, 28 April 1789. Bligh later reported: "Just before sun-rising, while I was yet asleep, Mr. Christian, with the master at arms, gunner's mate, and Thomas Burkett, seaman, came into my cabin, and seizing me, tied my hands with a cord behind my back, threatening me with instant death, if I spoke or made the least noise." Bligh claimed that he did cry out but the officers had already been secured and there were sentinels with muskets and bayonets.[101]

Christian only had a cutlass which was changed for a bayonet, while still holding Bligh. He brought the Captain to the deck and whenever he spoke, he was threatened with: "Hold your tongue sir, or you are dead this instant." Bligh noted that the men carrying muskets already had them cocked, ready to fire.

The small cutter had initially been put into the water with the clerk and two midshipmen but it immediately started to sink. Bailing was useless and such was the number of people set to leave the *Bounty*, Christian gave way to Mr. Cole's demands to have the largest launch.[102] The boatswain, carpenter and clerk Samuel were brought up to help and the boatswain was threatened "to take care of himself".

Quintal noticed Cole trying to wrench a ship's compass from the binnacle and demanded "What do you want with a compass with the land in sight?" Mutineer Burkett supported the request so Quintal let Cole take this prize. Tom Hayward appeared with a musket to take on the launch but Quintal snatched it: "Damn your eyes if you'll have that!"[103]

The boatswain and seaman were allowed "to collect twine, canvas, lines, sails, cordage, and 8 and 20 gallon casks of water". Mr Samuel was seeking Bligh's navigational aids and brought them onto the deck. Churchill challenged the clerk and allowed him to take the quadrant in addition to the compass and some papers. However, when he saw Samuel carrying the K2-timekeeper, maps, ephemeris, book of astronomical observations, sextant, surveys and drawings, he physically stopped Samuel on pain of death to touch them. "Damn your

---

[101] Bligh's Narrative, p96
[102] R Hough, The Bounty, p128
[103] Ibid, p136

eyes, you are well off to get what you have."[104] The mutineers had other plans for the K2 Bounty Watch.

Bligh later thanked Samuel in his account for saving what documents he could, including his commission, journals and some ships papers and particularly thanked his attempt 'to save the timekeeper'.

"Well then, can I have **K2** if I say *'please'*?"

Bligh tried to remonstrate with Christian, reminding him of past times, friendship, kindnesses and family relations which brought the famous response: "That, Captain Bligh – that is the thing – I am in hell – I am in hell."

The 18 loyalists in the boat were being subject to jeers, insults and threats while others called down pleading their innocence. Christian himself appeared to be the last to converse with Bligh and said, "Come Captain Bligh, your officers and men are now in the boat, and you must go with them; if you attempt to make the least resistance you will instantly be put to death." Bligh was forced over the side in his night gown and the launch was then set free. They drifted behind the *Bounty* where four

---

[104] Bligh's Narrative, p97

cutlasses were thrown to them. This particular act inspired the famous painting and engraving in 1790 by Robert Dudd in London.

Bligh was glad to be moving away from behind the *Bounty*. He was worried about musket fire in that position but even more worried about the *Bounty* being turned broadside on, enabling the four-pounder cannons to be trained on the launch.

Bligh sensibly rowed away as fast as possible, "towards Tofoa which bore ten leagues from us. While the *Bounty* was in sight it steered W N W which I considered as a feint since the cry ."Huzza for Otaheite" was frequently heard from the mutineers". Triumph was theirs.

> *These spurn their country with their rebel bark,*
> *And fly her as the raven fled the Ark,*
> *And yet they seek to nestle with their dove,*
> *And tame their fiery spirits down to love.*

Lord Byron

Chapter 10

They Went Their Ways
Bligh's Boat Journey
Finding Pitcairn 1790
Finding Mutineers 1791

The *Bounty* protagonists were splitting up. Captain Bligh and his 18 loyal sailors departed in their open launch, while the *Bounty*, under Fletcher Christian, sailed off to Tahiti carrying not only the mutineers, but also those loyalists for whom there was no room in the launch.

On arrival in Tahiti, this group split up yet again with the hard core of the mutineers sailing with Christian hoping to find 'Paradise' while the rest stayed in Tahiti, awaiting their fate. The long arm of Royal Navy justice would be sent out for them under Captain Edward Edwards in the *Pandora*, a 24-gun frigate.

Bligh's Open Boat Journey, 1789-90

In March 1790, Lieutenant William Bligh landed back in Portsmouth. On the way, he had plenty of time to consider his next step in England. He would have been aware that the mutiny would be a major event for the Navy and the public. He had already written to the Admiralty from Coupang, Timor, in August 1789, but it was important to have the public on his side and he was ready to publish his 'narrative' of this fatal voyage. This would precede a later 'account'.

Bligh published his narrative in 1790 and was determined to show himself in the best possible light in an event beyond his control. Image could be more important than substance. There would be two Courts Martial and the distinguished Lords would try to protect the Royal Navy's image to crown and country.[105]

Bligh's first priority was his own Court Martial on 22 October 1790, which was to examine him for losing the *Bounty* to 'pirates'. Bligh, his officers and some crew from the launch were questioned and there appeared to be some consensus about the events. The Admiralty had already received Bligh's limited written account from Coupang of the mutiny and open boat journey and he was honourably exonerated.

Bligh did, however, have the embarrassing task of personally apologising to the Admiralty for also losing the prized K2 Kendall timekeeper, which was the property of His Majesty and had cost the Admiralty the princely sum of £200, perhaps about £20,000 today.

Before the *Bounty* sailed, Bligh had confidently signed a receipt for K2 on 18 October 1787 for the Board of Longitude acknowledging the timekeeper and included: "which I promise to return to the maker on return".

It was, indeed, another matter on Bligh's actual return. On 27 October 1790, he wrote to the Admiralty,

"Sir, I am to inform you that the timekeeper, which was given to my charge on board His Majesty's Ship Bounty, was left in the said Ship when pirated from my command on 28 April 1790.
I have the honour to be Sir,
Your most Obedt, thy humble servant."

Bligh's public narrative was published before the *Pandora* under Captain Edwards sailed to the South Seas to round up the stranded crew and mutineers. After Bligh's long, dangerous 3,618 nautical mile open boat voyage with stops in Tofoa, the Barrier Reef, Coupang in Timor and Batavia, he finished his last page in the narrative with a flourish:

"On 14 March 1790, I was landed at Portsmouth by an Isle of Wight boat. FINIS"

Bligh defended himself along the lines of "The women of Otaheite are handsome, mild and cheerful in their manners and conversations, possessed of great sensibility, and have sufficient

---

[105] Bligh's Narrative, 1790, Nichols, London

delicacy to make them admired and beloved. The chiefs were so much attached to our people, that they rather encouraged their stay among them". It was "scarcely possible to have foreseen, that a set of sailors, most of them void of connections, should be led away". Many a man might be tempted!

Bligh must have boiled on the memory of how his clerk Samuel was roughly treated at bayonet point when trying to take a range of nautical instruments and papers and was even threatened with death.[106] The courageous clerk deserved Bligh's specific thanks for trying to save K2.[107]

The open launch was 23 feet long and about 6 foot 9 inches wide and it started off with 19 people including Bligh. He only lost John Norton, quartermaster, who was killed while fleeing from attacking natives where they had landed at Tofoa. With only four cutlasses and no muskets, the fear of cannibalism persuaded Bligh to limit future stops and go for a long haul to the Dutch East Indies.

The crew of the open boat were fortunate that Bligh was a master navigator. Bligh admitted having on board compass and quadrant for helping primarily with latitude. Documents included his commission, some material ship papers, navigational books but no charts. There was a watch belonging to gunner William Peckover, which continued to work for over a month. Bligh recorded the devastating moment "when unfortunately it stopped; so that noon, sun-rise, and sun-set, are the only parts of the 24 hours of which I can speak with certainty, as to time". Bligh must have craved for K2.

Bligh's account is already well known and covers the survival and relationships between the mariners in an historic and heroic voyage, which is still one of the longest open boat journeys in history.

In essence, just to get to Coupang in Timor in the Dutch East Indies, they incurred death in Tofoa, starvation, thirst, dangerous Polynesians and storms. Bligh managed to keep all but one loyalist alive and maintained discipline with some difficulty.

---

[106] Bligh's Log Book, p55–59. State Library of NSW, Australia
[107] Ibid, p59. Narrative

They only landed again at uninhabited points on the Great Barrier Reef.

Bligh continuously took navigational positions and used general terms such as "I considered", "I observed", "if I may judge". These comments must indicate that he regarded his positions as approximate. Longitudes and latitudes are impressively provided but apart from 'dead reckoning' he rarely specified his nautical tools.

Bligh on leaving the *Bounty* was "forbad on pain of death to touch...Sextant or Timekeeper or any of my drawings and surveys". In various reports and his early narrative and journal, he wrote when on the Barrier reef on 29 May that he had a "magnifying glass for lighting fires". Strangely, his later editions of his narrative changed his magnifying glass to "read off the divisions of my sextants".

Who changed it? It could have been Bligh but more likely his friend and legal adviser Captain James Burney who was entrusted to edit Bligh's accounts, particularly when he was away. His sister Fanny Burney kept a detailed personal diary in 1790 and indicated her brother's intense interest in Bligh's 'interesting narrative'. "Every word of which, James has taken to heart as if it were his own production."[108]

Bligh kept a 'Notebook' in 1789 during the launch journey which was only released a century and a half later. It proved that he also had a magnetic needle, a 10-inch Ramsden sextant and two books containing mathematical, astronomical and geographic information. This included Moore's 'Practical Navigator' and Maskelyne's 'Tables Requisite'. However, he didn't have his precious charts or a marine timekeeper.

Bligh's Notebook is a small leather bound signal book of 108 pages which originally belonged to Thomas Hayward, a favoured midshipman. Bligh noted on page 3: "This account was kept in my bosom." It was auctioned in 1976 and is now owned by the National Library of Australia.

When they finally arrived at Coupang in June/August 1789, they were well treated by the hospitable Dutch governor William Adrian Van Este, partly since Bligh could produce his Royal Navy commission to prove his story. Since they only had a few

---

[108] Fanny Burney Diaries. C Alexander, The Bounty, p179

half ducats, food, accommodation, clothing and ongoing journeys were only available on Royal Navy credit.

Bligh was anxious to return to England to tell his dramatic story to the world.

Finding Pitcairn. Mutineer's Dilemma, 1790

There were a number of survival options open to the mutineers. They knew they had at least a year. Probably 18 months. Possibly more. It would take this length of time for the Admiralty to respond to the mutiny. Bligh was cast adrift on 28 April 1789 arriving back in England in March 1790. Captain Edwards was subsequently sent to apprehend the *Bounty* mutineers, leaving England on 8 January 1791 and arriving in Tahiti on the *Pandora* on 9 May. The overall elapsed time was, indeed, just over two years.

The paucity of the mutineers' debate is puzzling. They just wanted to stay on an island in the Pacific. It could be inhabited or uninhabited, as long as it was in this region of the world. Fletcher Christian was educated and being the notional leader at this time, was in the best position to develop plans for a new life for him and his followers.

The American Revolutionary War had ended in September 1783, over four years before the *Bounty* left England and so the mutineers were fully aware that this vibrant new country called America was no longer under British rule and new immigrants were welcome. In the final battle of Yorktown, the British troops had fought bravely and loyally, but when the war was over, many successfully applied to join the new American army for better pay, conditions and a new life. The American navy actively protected British deserters.

The *Bounty's* tonnage was 215 tons, which was equivalent to the average sea-going whaler. The remaining *Bounty* crew were hardened sailors with a wide range of maritime experience and since the *Bounty* wasn't really equipped for whaling there was the easier sealing business. Some of the Tahitians could have been employed as extra hands.

Just one sealing expedition could have set them up financially, with or without their new wives, in the New World.

They were armed, could have sailed under new colours with a new ship's name and false identities, or claimed they were fleeing from 'British oppression'. If they couldn't sell the *Bounty,* they could have scuttled it off the east coast of America, got into prepared life boats and arrived as survivors of a tragic shipwreck. They could have applied for American citizenship.

Even Zephyrus, the Greek god of the west wind, was behind them to surge the *Bounty* around Cape Horn in the right direction. They had time. Risky? Yes, but all options were.

Once Bligh and his 18 companions had been decanted into the 23 foot launch and cast off, Christian and his new officers carried on in the *Bounty* to the cries of "Huzza for Otaheite". They continued on a WNW direction in an attempt to deceive the launch party.[109] In reality, the wind was not favourable for Tahiti so they decided to start with a two day sail to Tubuai instead.

Tubuai was about 300 miles to the south and was an optional new home for them, subject to friendly native relations. The locals were anything but friendly and it took musket and cannon volleys to disperse them. The mutineers thought that by leaving and returning with Tahitians as interpreters, the locals would be more welcoming. The *Bounty* then headed to Tahiti, which was another eight sailing days away.

There was an initial joyful welcome in Tahiti and the native chiefs were spun a story that Bligh was creating a new settlement and needed people and provisions. One version included having met up with Captain Cook again. As soon as there were sufficient volunteers and support, they tried to settle in Tubuai again.[110]

The natives were friendlier this time since they were able to communicate through the accompanying Tahitians. A fort was partially built for security but once again it all ended in gunfire and tears. After some vacillation, they returned to Tahiti where they were again well received by the local chiefs.

This was decision time! Christian pleaded with all the mutineers not to stay in Tahiti since it would result in certain capture.[111] The only alternatives on offer were trying to settle in the Marquesas Islands or find a completely different uninhabited

---

[109] Penguin Mutiny (BM), p242
[110] Ibid, p243
[111] Ibid, p244

island. Bligh's loyalists and the remaining mutineers in Tahiti would be left behind to wait for the British Navy.

One has to consider Christian's state of mind. One of the mutineers who remained in Tahiti said of Christian" "He hoped to live the remainder of his days without seeing the face of a European other than those who were already with him."[112]

The *Bounty's* ship papers included a copy of Hawkesworth's *Account of Voyages*, 1773, which included Carteret's account of the discovery of Pitcairn's Island in 1767 which confirmed it was 'uninhabited'.[113] Carteret's description included: "It was not more than five miles in circumference and seemed to be uninhabited. It was, however, covered with trees and we saw a small stream of fresh water running down one side of it." Further information included the island's isolation and difficulty of landing.

It must have sounded perfect to Christian who felt confident of finding Pitcairn's Island, possibly because he had retained Bligh's coveted K2-timekeeper. Although it is still debated whether Fletcher Christian knew how to navigate with K2 to find longitude, he probably did since Fletcher had good relations with Bligh in earlier voyages and early in this voyage. It is probable that Bligh would have quickly trained Fletcher on his latest navigational tool.

Provisions and stores were divided up between those staying for the Royal Navy and those sailing off in the *Bounty*. Those who favoured following Fletcher Christian included Young, Mills, Williams, Quintal, McCoy, Martin, Brown and Alex Smith. Brown was the assistant gardener who came to help with the bread fruit trees and sided with the mutineers. There were also six Polynesian men.

No further time was lost. There was some sort of party that night to which local women were invited and while most were dining or asleep, the *Bounty* cast off and drifted out to sea on the evening of 22 September 1789. "When the ship got about a mile outside the reefs (at least) one of the women leapt over board and

[112] James Morrison. Mutineer, A Sailor's Account, p70
[113] Carteret's Account. Hawkesworth Voyages, 1773, & R Hough, The Bounty, p198

swam ashore." Next morning, some of the elderly women were put ashore by canoe, while the younger ones were restrained from 'venturing to swim ashore' since several were inclined, being 'much afflicted at being torn from friends and relations'[114]

This was a catastrophe for most of those young girls and women being unwillingly wrenched from their lives and homes and divided up as chattels, by strange hardened men. This kidnapping is just one more chapter in the long history of man's inhumanity to woman.

Each of the nine white mutineers had or chose their selected female. Fletcher Christian had his existing beloved partner Isabella and Mathew Quintal also brought his Sarah. The other seven mutineers seemed content with their lot. One Polynesian man had his own partner while the other five shared two unfortunate females. It didn't need a crystal ball to predict there was trouble ahead.

The *Bounty* travelled through the Friendly Islands and carried out some trade with local natives in canoes, but Christian was determined that he could only consider stopping at a completely uninhabited location, so pushed on towards the mapped location of Pitcairn. This took about two months. Christian had the benefit of K2 and although it was not as accurate as K1, it was far better than any navigational instruments that Captain Carteret used. Based on Carteret's latitude 25°2'S and longitude 133° 21'W, they discovered that Pitcairn's Island just wasn't there. It was lost at sea!

Frustration was building up, so Christian may have decided that Carteret's latitude was more likely to be accurate than his longitude. At last, one evening, they found Pitcairn's Island, the great towering rock, which matched Carteret's drawings.

The Island was nearly 200 miles out from Carteret's longitude's position. Christian must have been elated with this additional security. The Admiralty would be slow in changing their maps and future navigators seeking Pitcairn would have modern timekeepers and would be looking some 200 miles away.

---

[114] Jenny's Story. Mutineer's wife, Penguin BM, p228

It was 15 January 1790, about nine months after the mutiny that they found Pitcairn. Because of foul weather, they couldn't land for three days. When conditions improved, Christian brought the *Bounty* nearer the shore to lower the cutter. Christian, Brown, Williams, McCoy and three Polynesian men carefully rowed to a narrow beach. All were armed.[115] "The crew reported that there were no natives on the island; that it abounded with cocoa-nuts and sea fowl."

Further good news was that there were signs of previous inhabitants, which proved the island could support human life. They found "charcoal, stone axes, stone foundations of houses with a few carved boards".

The mutineers started stripping the *Bounty* and brought over what they could in small boats and rafts. Tents were made from sails and were erected for providing temporary cover and with open fires they cooked a large hog. Houses would be hidden from ships at sea by the verdant foliage.

There were reports that Christian was happier than he had been for a long time and there was discussion about the fate of the *Bounty*. Christian "wanted to save her for a while" but others insisted on burning her immediately and did so on 23 January 1790.[116]

"During the night all were in tears at seeing her in flames. Some regretted exceedingly they had not confined Captain Bligh and returned to their native country, instead of acting as they had done."[117]

It would be eighteen long years before they and K2 were discovered.

Finding Mutineers. Captain Edward Edwards, RN 1791

The Admiralty didn't wait for long to seek out and capture the *Bounty* mutineers to face Royal Navy justice. The frigate

---

[115] Ibid
[116] John Adams Story. Penguin BM, p245
[117] Jenny's Story.

Pandora sailed from Portsmouth on 7 November 1790 with 134 crew including Lieutenant Thomas Haywood who had been a midshipman on the *Bounty* with his close friend midshipman Peter Heywood, who was now deemed a mutineer.

The *Pandora* surgeon George Hamilton noted: "Officers and men received six months' pay in advance and after receiving their final orders, got the timekeeper on board, weighed anchor and proceeded to sea"[118].

Captain Edwards had been very carefully selected as a reliable disciplinarian. His orders were crystal clear:

"You are to keep the mutineers as closely confined as may preclude all possibility of their escaping, having however, proper regard to the preservation of their lives that they may be brought home to undergo the punishment due to their demerits."[119]

Edwards would be unaware that the mutineers had dispersed and that part of the group was already ensconced in their Pitcairn's Island hideout and sanctuary. The *Pandora* sailed via Cape Horn and saw Easter Island before ironically, passing 300 miles from Pitcairn Island. They finally reached Tahiti on 23 March 1791.

An excited Peter Heywood swam out to the *Pandora* followed by two others who were all immediately clamped in irons in an open cage on deck, subsequently called 'Pandora's Box'. It was about 3.4 x 5.5 metres wide for all 14 prisoners including the nearly blind fiddler, Michael Byrne.

Lieutenant Thomas Haywood was now an officer and led some of the teams to capture the 'pirates'. Steadily they were rounded up including a small schooner, which was a planned escape vessel. Some were hunted down with native help while others surrendered.

There was much distress on the *Pandora's* decks with the men's wives and girlfriends wailing in sorrow and cutting their faces, knowing they would never see their men again.

---

[118] Voyage Round the World, George Hamilton. He mentioned that Lt Hayward came on board with a timekeeper, but didn't specify which one
[119] Captain Edward's Orders, ADM 2120

There is a heart wrenching story of Peggy; a beautiful pregnant Tahitian girl who had to be forcibly torn from her lover's chained arms. He was young midshipman Stewart who requested she not be admitted on board again because of the mutual tears and stress. Some years later, missionaries vouched that she had died of a broken heart. Coincidentally, her death was just a few weeks before Stewart drowned in the sinking *Pandora*, still chained to his prison and unable to escape. Happily, the missionaries brought up the 'mixed blood' child, but it is a South Pacific 'Romeo and Juliet'.[120]

On 8 May, Captain Edwards with his crew and prisoners left Tahiti to hunt down Christian and the remaining mutineers. Over 3 months they visited new and old islands without success. So near yet so far! It was time to leave.

They returned home taking the western route via the Torres Strait. Being aware that they were sailing near 'coral' waters, Edwards put out in daylight a small boat to feel the way. This was to no avail and on 29 August 1791 *Pandora* went aground at dawn on the Great Barrier Reef and rapidly started to founder. The pumps couldn't keep up.

The *Pandora* Founders on the Barrier Reef 1791

---

[120] Voyage of HMS Pandora, Intro, p8, Basil Thompson, 1915

Most of the 14 prisoners were still chained to their 'Box'. Captain Edwards gave no orders to 'release the prisoners'. Fortunately, the master-at-arms supported by William Moulter, a boatswain's mate, took personal risks and passed the keys to the desperate, clutching prisoners.[121] Even so, four of the 'pirates' didn't have enough time and sank with the ship in the company of the humane master-at-arms and many others.

Eighty-nine crew and 10 prisoners were picked up by four boats and landed on a sand bank four miles away. Thirty-four crew and 4 mutineers drowned. Edwards ensured there was no relief for the surviving mutineers. The wrecking led to a survival voyage comparable to Bligh's but with four boats instead of one large launch. This shorter voyage is already well documented but essentially, they suffered the expected problems of thirst, hunger, danger and other privations.

The prisoners were split across the four boats to ensure there were not enough of them to take over any one boat. This eleven hundred miles survival journey lasted to mid-September 1791, when they too reached Coupang and Timor and received another kind Dutch reception. They were met by Mr Frey, the lieutenant governor, who took Captain Edwards and Lieutenant Haywood to meet Governor Mynheer Vanjon.[122]

Once again, the fact that Captain Edward had his officer's commission and documentary proof meant that he could operate with Royal Navy credit, unlike the recent arrival of another group of shipwrecked Europeans, who turned out to be escaped Australian convicts, which is another story.

By another coincidence, explorer Amasa Delano also arrived at Timor Island soon after the *Pandora* party had left and was again kindly received by Mr Frey and Governor Vanjon and was shown by Vanjon a draft copy of Edward's history of the *Pandora* voyage to date.

Delano made his own copy and later met up with his American mariner friend Mayhew Folger, with whom he had previously speculated about the fate of the *Bounty* mutineers and who later became part of the K2 story. [123]

---

[121] Ibid, Notes G, Hamilton, p74
[122] Narrative Amasa Delano, 1817, Ch. V.
[123] Ibid, p37

Captain Edwards' report of 25 November 1791 is a remarkable document and although it was a defensive report for his court martial, it also illustrated his skills as a mariner and navigator. He produced a list of the locations of over 50 ports and islands headed by "The Latitudes and Longitudes of the different places touched at or discovered by his majesty's ship *Pandora*, taken with the greatest accuracy from the centre of the islands"[124].

The Court Martial of the mutineers commenced on 12 September 1792 on the *Duke* for ten mutineers. In summary, four were acquitted, six were found guilty of mutiny, of which one was acquitted on appeal, two received a King's pardon two months later, and the other three were hanged.

The two pardoned prisoners apparently seemed reasonably relaxed in the trials. Young Heywood had youth and connections on his side while Morrison came over well in the trials and appeared to deliberately concentrate his bile on Edwards rather than Bligh.

Author Donald Maxton wrote "There was already a good deal of unrest in the ranks of the Royal Navy" and "the establishment would not want to risk a scandal".[125]

Royal Navy executions of mutineers were often designed to be high drama and a public spectacle. These executions took place on 29 October 1792 on the *Brunswick* at Portsmouth, where a contingent from each ship in the harbour attended the executions.

The three prisoners had nooses placed around their necks and were then pulled up alive into the masts and spars, for the ship's crews and a festive audience to see and absorb the full horror.

Explorer Amasa Delano had studied mutinies and concluded in 1817:

"I have known more than twenty instances, where crews have attempted to do themselves justice by violent measures against their commanders, and in every one of them, the departure from subordination and obedience uniformly increased the evil and led to the most unhappy consequences."

---

[124] Voyage HMS Pandora, G Hamilton Narrative, 1793, p171
[125] DA Maxton, p6, Edit Morrison & Heywood's writing

"Probably it is best without a single exception for the sufferers to wait till they are on shore and can have a regular trial by proper authorities, before they attempt to seek a remedy in any other way."[126]

---

[126] Narrative Amasa Delano, Ch V1 Reflections

Royal Observatory, Greenwich c. 1870

Pitcairn Island – Lost at Sea

Sir Cloudesley Shovell

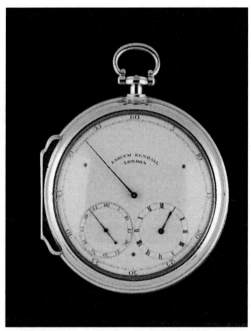

Larcum Kendall's Timekeeper K2 – 1771

Nelson Fighting White Bear

The *Asia* in Halifax Harbour 1797

Admiral Robert Digby (1732–1815)

The Coming of the Loyalists

A Chart of the Western Coast of Africa

Portrait of Rear Admiral William Bligh

Matavai Bay, Tahiti

The Bounty

Bligh leaving the *Bounty*

Bounty Voyages Map

New Guinea

Coupang

Australia

Endeavour Strait

Tasmania

New Zealand

Pacific Ocean

Tofua

Palmerston

Tubuai

Tahiti

Pitcairn

- - - Voyage of Bounty prior to mutiny
——— Voyage of Bounty after mutiny and finding Pitcairn
.... Voyage of Bligh in longboat

PART TWO
K2 Pitcairn Recovery
1807

Chapter 11
Nantucket's Ocean Harvest

In April 1807, eighteen years after the *Bounty* mutineers landed at Pitcairn carrying K2, a young Quaker Nantucket sea captain called Mayhew Folger was preparing for his 2nd southern sealing expedition. Generations of the Folger family had lived off the sea and Mayhew was continuing the tradition.

Nantucket Island is just south of Cape Cod and their seamen had a particularly high reputation for whaling and sealing in 1807. Their sons would either sail on their own whalers and sealers or command ships for other owners.

The name 'Cape Cod' is perfect. The Pilgrim Fathers, who came over in the Mayflower in the 17th century, would never have claimed they could walk on water. However, many believed they could walk on the backs of the prime cod fish packed into these waters.

**An Island in Time. A Native American Legend Explaining
Nantucket's Origins**

Once upon a time, there lived on the Atlantic coast a giant who used Cape Cod for a bed. One night, being restless, he tossed from side to side till his moccasins were filled with sand. This so enraged him that on rising in the morning he flung the offending moccasins from his feet, one to form Martha's Vineyard, the other became the famous island of Nantucket.

The Glacier's Gift, E Folger, 1911.

Quaker families were comfortable with the local Indians who were already living well off the sea and they noted their skills in hunting, killing and retrieving in-shore whales. These native inhabitants used the geographic advantage of Nantucket to the full. Close-shore whales would be chased from canoes and hooked with javelins tipped with 'bone made' hooks. Once fixed, the thrashing whales would be finished off by continuous spearing with javelins and arrows.

The dead or nearly dead whale would then be dragged ashore where a whole village would carve up the carcase for meat, blubber and anything else of use. It would be a time of celebration and a time to respect the soul of the departed whale.

The Quaker families were generally humane, committed and honourable people who combined their beliefs with outstanding business enterprise, in those opportunities actually allowed to them. They employed many of the local Indians who were lethal when using the modern metal tipped harpoons. Herman Melville illustrated mixed crews such as harpooner Queequeg, in his classic *Moby-Dick*, later published in 1851.

From 1650, a group of established Quaker families extended the coastal whale hunt into deeper, distant waters. The Society of Friends quickly became widely renowned in this new oil business. Whale oil!

Moby Dick

Queequeg

The main hunt was for right whales, hump backs and the valuable sperm whale, Physeter macrocephalus. The demand for oil increased over the next 100 years for lamps, lubrication, leather softening and varied other trades.

Sperm oil was particularly valuable, since it gave a clearer light with less smoke and fumes. The 200 litres of Spermaceti oil within the great skull of the Sperm whale was the finest of all oils. It was suggested in *Moby-Dick* that it was part of the battering ram of a monstrous-sized beast.

This prime oil changed into wax when exposed to the air and made luxurious candles for gracing the tables of high society. It was also the favourite fuel for life-saving coastal light houses. Ambergris was another valuable by-product, formed when countless sharp squid beaks have been crushed and pocketed away in the sperm whale's guts. It is still valued today, as a fixing agent in perfumes and as a spice in the Far East.

During this period, whaling boats and schooners increased in size and facilities. The vessels ranged between 50 and 600 tons and boiling blubber into oil in metal try-works became an 'on-board', rather than an 'on-shore' function.

In 1750, Nantucket was dominant in the whaling market with 60 sloops, but fierce competition grew from other American ports such as New Bedford, Boston and New York. Even more competition came from British, French, Spanish, Dutch and Portuguese whalers.

London was the main market for whale oil. There was a close commercial working relationship between London and the American East Coast whaling centres, of which Nantucket was the most important. This relationship was even closer in the Seven Years War when there was a common enemy. French warships combining with French and Spanish privateers harassed both colonial American and British commercial shipping.

In 1778, the price of Sperm oil on the London market increased to £40.00 per tonne, providing Nantucket with product revenue of £150,000 per annum.

New whaling grounds were needed to satisfy demand and to support the bigger international whaling fleets, so enterprising New England whalers spread out in an ocean wide search. Just before the War of Independence, 26,000 of the 40,000 barrels of Sperm oil taken by the whole whale fishery of Massachusetts were from Nantucket.[127]

The American War of Independence 1775–1783 played havoc with the New England whaling fleets. Previous close families, friends and allies turned into enemies in a long, bitter and emotional war. Nantucket's registered fleet of about 125 ships in 1775 was nearly all destroyed, including cargoes valued at $500,000.

It was a personal and political dilemma for Quaker families. Although whaling is a brutal business, Societies of Friends tend to be pacifist when dealing with their fellow man. It is against their culture to take up arms to kill people, which is a precarious stance in war.

Nantucket did attempt neutrality, which made their new Continental Congress distrustful. The British restraining orders of 1775[128] and Navigation Acts forced Nantuckers to negotiate

---

[127] Walter Hayes, The Captain from Nantucket, William Clements Library

[128] Edward Stackpole, Sea Hunters, p66

with Britain while the colonial local government was determined that Britain should not gain any useful supplies through Nantucket. The British granted a limited number of whaling licences, to ensure this exposed community could earn a living.

Nantucket whalers were in demand worldwide, because of their experience and skills in harvesting the valuable Sperm whale, when European whalers were still concentrating on the smaller bony 'Right' whales. Competing countries were offering citizenship, compensation and guarantees of religious freedom to these Quakers. The British initially wanted the whalers moved to Nova Scotia, where some of their brethren had moved some years earlier.

At the end of the century, there were four international centres of whaling excellence where Nantucket families had migrated to: New England USA, Nova Scotia Canada, Newport Wales, and Dunkirk France.

This war also interrupted the new maritime business of worldwide commercial sealing. After the war, young Mayhew Folger with other leading mariner families pursued a new 'Seal Rush' which later played a pivotal part in rediscovering the lost *Bounty* mutineers and the lost K2-timekeeper.

From about 1750 to 1850, there was a frenzied increase in worldwide hunting for this easy money. Seal products became another international business and just as the 'Gold Rush' generated intensive searches for new gold fields, similar efforts focussed on discovering new seal fields.

These frenetic opportunities attracted small players as well as large enterprises. Although some existing whale hunters included the harvesting of seals in their expeditions, there was a lower cost of entry for those focussing on seals alone. The pressure of discovering new seal rookeries before other hunters led to the discovery of new islands. American historian E Stackpole called these mariners "nomads of the sea".

Unlike the Inuit in Nantucket, who appeared to believe that all earthly living things have souls, the mass hunters in 1750 were remorseless and without restraint, until the pragmatic efforts of conservation from the 1850s onwards.[129]

---

[129] Ibid, Part Two

This was a great era of ocean exploration and reports from sea captains, such as Dampier, Anson, Delano and Cook, had an impact on the growth of seal hunting which accelerated this rush of exploitation.

William Dampier was a successful buccaneer and explorer who reported in 1683 about the seals in the Pacific Juan Fernandez Islands: "Here are always thousands, I might possibly say millions of them, either sitting on the bays, or going and coming in the sea around the island, which is full of them. When they come out of the sea, they bleat like Sheep for their young…and will not suffer any to suck." Only fur seals bleat like sheep.[130]

Commodore George Anson was a British naval commander in 1740-44, who was sent with a small squadron to the Pacific to attack Spanish possessions at the start of the War of Austrian Succession. He also stopped at Juan Fernandez Islands to obtain fresh goat and seal meat to help fight scurvy, before continuing his exploration and quest for Spanish treasure. He recorded: "The grass would prove a dainty and was all eagerly devoured. The seals were also considered as fresh provision."[131]

The Ice Islands: Cook in Antarctica 1773

---

[130] Dampier, A new Voyage Round the World, 1697, revised 1703, vol. 1, pp 88, 90
[131] Henry Elliot, Seal Islands of Alaska, p119, 120

The three voyages of Captain Cook became internationally famous and his discovery of South Georgia on his 2nd voyage probably had the biggest impact on global sealing. Cook reported: "Not a tree or shrub to be seen – not big enough for a toothpick – but teaming with seals."[132] New rookeries were like gold mines and Cook's discoveries were known.

Although disappointed that South Georgia was not part of the Antarctic continent, Cook claimed the island for King George. The ceremony involved raising the Union Jack flag, followed by three volleys of musket fire, which terrified and scattered the witnessing penguins and seals.

Amasa Delano was the explorer and mariner who had the most impact on Folger and the recovery of the lost K2-timekeeper. His news and reports of the size of seal populations in the South Pacific highlighted an opportunity for even small teams to make a fortune.

Delano met the Nantucket captain Mayhew Folger, who was on his 1st sealing expedition in the schooner *Minerva*, at the island of Mas Afuera in 1800. They got on exceedingly well and regularly socialised over a few drinks. Delano later reported "His Company was particularly agreeable to him".[133] They both seemed sympathetic to the story of the *Bounty* mutineers, "they were alive to the anxieties and distresses of mind under the circumstances of Christian's going from all that he had loved"[134].

Delano had been able to update Folger in their initial talks in 1800, since in 1791 he had stayed several days in Timor where Bligh had landed after his historic long sea voyage in an open boat. Indeed, he stayed in the same comfortable accommodation that Bligh had occupied.

Timor was also the port that Captain Edwards later landed with 10 *Bounty* mutineer prisoners after the ship-wrecking of the *Pandora*, which had been sent to arrest the mutineers. Edwards left his draft voyage report with the Dutch governor, who in turn lent it to Delano who made his own copy. This news was exciting which he discussed with Folger in 1800, concluding, "We were

---

[132] Cook's Journals, 2nd Voyage
[133] Quarterly Review, 1815. Delano's Voyages, 1817
[134] Ibid

both much interested to know what ultimately became of Christian, his ship and his party."

Ten years later, Delano made a point of meeting up with Captain Folger in Boston after 1810 following Folger's re-discovery of Pitcairn's Island, the mutineers and K2, so he could take copious notes while memories were fresh in Folger's mind. They further corresponded in 1816 which gave more material for Delano's *Narratives* in 1817.

Delano made a fortune and was reputed to have sold 100,000 seal skins in Canton over a seven year period. He mainly hunted at Mas Afuera. The skins would be held in warehouses or 'Kongs' in China until sold. The average price was about $1 per skin. That money could then be exchanged for tea, silks and quality porcelain (china!) and any other luxury goods, which could be profitably sold in America or Europe.

Folger's ship on this historic next voyage in 1807, is often called a 'whaler'. Although built as a whaler, it is important to emphasise in this story that it was on a sealing expedition. Whalers travel across oceans and currents seeking swimming whales, usually in ocean waters. In the case of sealers, they were deliberately seeking out islands in the search of new rookeries, since most seals are land based.

Folger had, like most secretive sealers, studied the latest information from explorers and old maps. Folger specifically identified Pitcairn Island in the South Pacific from Carteret's reports, which described it as "uninhabited" so he could well be the first sealer there.

In April 1807, Folger was continuing to prepare his sealer-hunter ship.

He might be lucky in also harvesting some Sea Otters with their luxurious fur, containing 650,000 tiny fur hairs per square inch.[135] However, his prime targets were fur and elephant seals.

Captain Mayhew Folger knew that he was in an international race to find seal colonies on new beaches and islands. If he hadn't been a sealer, he would never have re-discovered Pitcairn's Island and who knows what could have happened to K2?

---

[135] Briton Busch, The war against seals p.2

Epilogue 'The Killing Fields' chapter provides more information about both the business and hunting sides of seals in the 18th and 19th centuries. Readers are advised that it covers some aspects of the brutality of historic seal hunting.

Chapter 12
Captain Folger's Ocean Desert
1807

On April 5, 1807, Captain Mayhew Folger sailed out from New Bedford in his ship the *Topaz* on a major new seal hunting voyage. It was a fully rigged three-masted ship. Knowing he would be away for some years, he was probably emotional sailing past Martha's Vineyard Island and particularly his home and birthplace, Nantucket Island. He discharged his local pilot on the same day, before venturing into the Atlantic.

He was seeking existing, new and undiscovered seal rookeries. Only by finding them teeming with seals could he turn them into valuable killing fields.

Other hunting teams from New England ports and Europe, were competing. Some were friends. Some were foes. Mayhew would have remembered the success of his 1st sealing voyage command and been eager to match it. It was then in October 1799 and was in the Salem-based sealing boat *Minerva*. He was then just 25 years old but already a hardened sailor and well regarded in his local Quaker community.

Feeding on the experience of earlier voyages and knowledge of his friends, he planned to head straight to the South Pacific and concentrate on St Mary's and Mas Afuera in the Juan Fernandez group of islands, where he had been so successful in 1799–1800.

This is where Alexander Selkirk, upon whom Daniel Defoe is commonly supposed to have modelled Robinson Crusoe, had been marooned for more than four years from 1704. Katherine Frank in 'Crusoe' appears to expose the story as a myth. She purports that Defoe based his book on several castaways, including Robert Knox from his Sri Lankan experience and Defoe's own adventures. The Victorian critic Leslie Stephen was also quoted with his own Crusoe summary: "Robinson Crusoe is Defoe and more than Defoe, for he is the typical Englishman of his time."[136]

Selkirk was rescued on 2 February 1709 by Captain Woodes Rogers in his privateer, the *Duke*. Rogers noted that Selkirk babbled on about the multitudes of seals and goats when rescued from the island. Although goats play a big part in Defoe's Crusoe novel, seals mysteriously do not.

This privateer was piloted by explorer William Dampier, who after a brief time, appointed Selkirk to 2nd mate. Selkirk was fit and invaluable from the beginning in helping to outrun and catch goats for fresh meat to help the crew's fight against scurvy. His later fame inspired a number of poems and possibly the best known is this first verse by William Cowper:

The Solitude of Alexander Selkirk.

"I am the monarch of all I survey;
My right there is none to dispute.
From the centre all 'round to the sea,
I am the lord of the fowl and the brute,
Solitude! Where are the charms
That sages have seen in thy face?
Better dwell in the midst of alarms,
Than reign in this horrible place."

These islands are also the place Mayhew Folger met and developed a friendship with the explorer Amasa Delano from Massachusetts in his sealer *Perseverance*. Delano wrote of his new drinking companion: "we were often relating to each other our adventures...the fate of the *Bounty* was several times introduced[137]. Mayhew no doubt hoped to meet up again on this current trip.

Folger's 1st voyage had been a financial success. The islands were heaving with seals. Once his ship, the *Minerva*, was packed

---

[136] Crusoe "the Creation of a Myth", Katherine Frank p81–82
[137] Delano, p138

with fur seal skins, he had steered across the Pacific to Canton. His return to Salem in May 1802 produced a profit of $40,000 for the owners and gave Mayhew Folger the money to marry his sweetheart, Mary Joy, back in Nantucket.

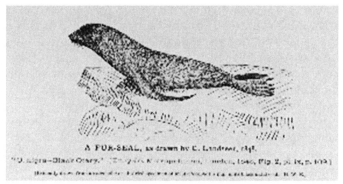

A Fur Seal. C Landseer 1848

In the six years since his 1st sealing expedition, none of Folger's voyages had produced comparable profits. This new voyage, however, was Folger's 2nd sealing expedition. His command in the converted whaling ship *Topaz*, registered in Boston, was a big opportunity for him. As he sailed from New Bedford on his voyage of destiny, he confidently logged on 5 April 1807 that he was "Bound to the South Seas and Canton"[138].

Although sealing catches hadn't yet peaked, Mayhew would be well aware that some of the better known fields were already heavily exploited and sometimes virtually destroyed. In 1799, Captain Fenning in another sealer had great success in the Juan Fernandez islands when he shipped 100 tons of seal skins to Canton. He claimed: "he left 500-700,000 seals behind."[139] That was no guarantee in 1807.

Although he would head in that direction, it would be the discovery of new fields that could produce spectacular profits, but it was risky. The first step was to cross the Atlantic to Cape Verde Islands off the coast of NW Africa. This was a good source of salt for drying fur skins and he bought 2,200 bushels.

---

[138] Topaz Log Book, Nantucket Historical Assoc
[139] Seal Islands, Dept Interior, HW Elliott, p117

Amasa Delano emphasised the importance of effective drying of seal skins before storage. Apart from quality, damp furs attracted rats. He even logged his dismay, when a rat ran off with one of his shoes. A courageous rat!

The log book of the *Topaz* illustrates a journey of one disaster after another. Returning across the Atlantic, they landed in Trinidad off Brazil to take on water on 14 June 1807 only to have one of the two boats stoved, which forced him to look elsewhere. On 21 July, he logged: "Very heavy Gales of wind and a tremendous Sea such as I have very rarely seen in the course of my peregrinations and the water sifting in every part of the upper works, which makes it very disagreeable..."

It would be worrying that Mayhew had taken over two months crossing the Atlantic and back again, without any profit. He then made a reasonable decision to go to the South Atlantic. He reached the Falklands area in early August and was "well assured that no land exists nearer than South Georgia". His immediate concern was the weather.

He then turned east but "severe gales of wind and as heavy a fall of snow" combined with "a confused sea" made his position untenable, particularly when one of his boats was unusable. Even his sextant would have been difficult to use so his compass may have been his best friend. By the time he saw Desolation (Kerguelen) Island towards the end of September 1807, over five months had passed and had nothing to show for it.

There were probably good hunting opportunities on Desolation Island at this time but his log book refers to "bad seas" and "snowing very fast". The sleet appeared to be a major discomfort since the cabins and holds were continuously damp. This would be exacerbated by the chill factor of bitterly freezing winds with icicle fingers searching a way through the very stitches in clothing. Mayhew then decided in October to sail to Van Diemen's Land (Tasmania) to find wood and fresh water in Adventure Bay.[140] Over 6 months and still not a single seal skin.

There was clear relief when Folger arrived in Tasmania and was able to anchor in about 12 fathoms over a firm sandy bottom. They were able to collect water and firewood to dry out their bones, as well as their clothes and ship.

---

[140] Topaz Log Book, 1807, NHA

Despite the conflict of the American Revolutionary war and the destruction of most of the Nantucket whaling and sealing fleets, Mayhew Folger seemed comfortable in dealing with officers of the Royal Navy. It may have been his warm personality or the mutual respect of maritime nations. However, on October 24 the British *Porpoise* appeared while the *Topaz* was anchored and fired some greeting salutes.

The commander, Captain Scott, came on board seeking to purchase supplies, so Folger "agreed to accompany him up the river Derwent to a new town called Hobart". On arrival, the commander of the *Porpoise* once again fired his greeting shots to the small town. They met up with the local Governor, David Collins, who was in charge of the small settlement of about 800 people which included 225 prisoners.

Folger apparently sold 420 gallons of gin and rum to the *Porpoise* for "the ship's use".[141] Morale soared. Three weeks later, Folger headed for Chatham Islands where he had been warned about 'dangerous natives' in the area. He finally got lucky on 23 November at a nearby rocky area off Pitt Island, where they stayed for two days in a small rookery while they despatched and skinned 600 seals.[142] They were on their way.

In mid-December, Folger reached the Antipodes Islands near the southern end of New Zealand. There, he found sealing teams but no seals. Although the seal rush was still thriving, known colonies of seals were already becoming endangered. He had to find new rookeries.

Because of the appalling weather, Folger had been unlucky in not being able to exploit the existing fields in the Shetlands and South Georgia. Unfortunately, he was just too early for the subsequent discovery of lucrative new seal colonies in Macquarie's Islands, to the south of Tasmania.

Folger's urgency was understandable. While at Antipodes Island on 18 December 1807, Folger logged:

"No seals to be found, proceeding to Pitcairn Island, thought to be uninhabited and a possible site for sealing."

---

[141]Seal Islands, Dept Interior, HW Elliott, p117
[142] Delano, p138

Folger would have studied every trace of islands before setting off. He had clearly read about Carteret's voyage and furthermore, Pitcairn's Island was by now shown on the latest printed ocean maps. Captain Carteret had declared the island "destitute of inhabitants". Perfect!

The plan was particularly attractive to Folger, since he could try to find Pitcairn's Island and still be roughly on course for the Juan Fernandez group of islands off Chile.

Folger's mind was made up. He decided that his next immediate objective was finding Pitcairn's Island. He had Carteret's maps and locations, so being southeast of New Zealand he "put the ship on an east north east course, gradually describing an arc and heading due north"[143], only to find that Carteret's navigation was wrong.

Being comfortable with his latitude, Folger had to make a decision to turn west or east to find the true longitude for Pitcairn. Right and east would keep him on track for Juan Fernandez, but could lose any feasible chance of finding Pitcairn. Left and west would take him further away from the main sealing colonies, but could give him another chance of finding Pitcairn, when returning. Folger chose west – towards Pitcairn's Island and his page in history.

---

[143] The Sea Hunters, EA Stackpole, p240

Chapter 13
Rediscovering Pitcairn's Island
1808 K2 Recovered

Log Book of Ship *Topaz*, Captain Mayhew Folger, Saturday, 6 February 1808:

"First part light airs at East. Stearing W B S ½ S by compass at ½ past 1 PM saw landing bearing S W B W ½ W. Steered for the land with a light breeze at East the said land being Pitcairn Island discovered in 1767 by Captain Carteret in his Britannic Majesty's sloop Swallow."[144]

"At 2 AM the Isle Bore South 2 leagues dis. Lay off & on till daylight, at 6 AM put off with 2 boats to Explore the land and look for seals. On approaching the Shore saw a smoke on the land at which I was very much Surprised it being represented by Capt Carteret as destitute of inhabitants, on approaching Still nearer the land – I discovered a Boat paddling towards me with 3 men in her. On approaching her they hailed in the English language asked who was Captain of the Ship."[145]

"Who are you?"

"This is the ship *Topaz* of the United States of America. I am the master, Captain Mayhew Folger an American."

"You are an American? You come from America? Where is America? Is it in Ireland?"

"Who are you?"

---

[144] Journal Topaz, Saturday, 6 February 1808, Captain Mayhew Folger

[145] Delano, Narrative, 1817, p139. He wrote Aleck for Alec in the landing. Folger spent months with the explorer Delano on a seal hunt in 1800. Delano wrote to Folger in June 1816 and met up again in Boston before publishing

"We are Englishmen."

"Where were you born?"

"On that island which you can see."

"How can you be Englishmen if you were born on that island, which the English do not own and never possessed?"

"We are Englishmen because our father is an Englishman."

"Who is your father?"

"Aleck..."

"Who is Aleck?"

"Don't you know Aleck?"

"How should I know Aleck?"

"Well then, do you know Captain Bligh of the *Bounty*?"

At this question, Folger later told explorer Delano: "That the whole story immediately burst upon his mind, and produced a shock of mingled feelings, surprise, wonder and pleasure, not to be described."

The man speaking to Folger was the seventeen-year-old son of Fletcher Christian usually called 'Thursday'. Folger was absolutely clear to Delano and believed he had been asked of America: **"Is it in Ireland?"** However, bearing in mind the men were in different moving boats, there is a view that young Thursday was asking about America: **"Is it an island?"** This is probable since all the youngsters and all their South Pacific mothers would never have seen any land other than islands.

"They offer me a number of cocoanuts which they had Brought off as a present, and requested I would land, there being as they said a white man on shore."[146]

Delano quoted Folger: "The canoe returned with a message that Aleck would not come on board the ship since the women were fearful of his safety but extended an invitation for Captain Folger to come on shore. The young men pledged themselves to Captain Folger that he had nothing to apprehend if he should land." A later undated letter from Samuel Coates describing a meeting with his friend Folger in Philadelphia indicated that one

---

[146] Topaz Log Book, 6 February 1808

of Folger's sailors, John Brown, was first to actually land to confer with Aleck Smith.[147]

"After this negotiation, Folger was determined to go on shore and as he landed he was met by Aleck and all his family and was welcomed with every demonstration of joy and good will. They escorted him from the shore to the house of their patriarch, where every luxury they had was set before him and offered with the most affectionate courtesy.

Mayhew Folger

"Smith informed me that after putting Captain Bligh in the long boat and sending her adrift their commander – Christian proceeded to Otaheite, there all the mutineers chose to stop except Christian himself & seven others, they all took wives at Otaheite and six men as servants and proceeded to Pitcairn Island where they landed all goods and chattels, ran the Ship *Bounty* on shore and Broke her up. This took place as near as he could recollect 1790 soon after which one of their party ran mad and drowned himself. Another died with a fever, and after they had

---

[147] Letter (1811–1813) from Samuel Coates after meeting Folger

remained about 4 years on the Island, their Men servants rose upon & killed Six of them. Leaving only Smith alive and he desperately wounded with a pistol ball in the neck.

"However, he and the widows of the deceased arose and put all the Servants to death which left him the only Surviving man on the Island with 8 or 9 women and Several Small Children. He Immediately went to work tilling the ground so it produced plenty for them all and he lives very comfortably as Commander in Chief of Pitcairn's Island."

Aleck was, of course, the mutineer Alexander Smith who informed Folger that "they lived under Fletcher Christian's government for several years after they landed; that during the whole period they enjoyed tolerable harmony; that Christian became sick and died a natural death; and it was after this that the Otaheitan men joined in a conspiracy and killed the English husbands of the Otaheitan women and were by the widows killed in turn on the following night. Eventually, Smith was thus the only man left on this island."

A number of other ships followed after *Topaz* left Pitcairn and all fundamentally relied on information from Alexander Smith, who by then had adopted the name of John Adams. The stories Smith would tell these visitors varied – including the specifics of how Christian died. But Mayhew Folger was the first to hear them, having discovered the mutineer's colony when Smith's memories were freshest. Delano confirmed in his writings that the information from Captain Folger was worthy of confidence. Delano continued: "Smith had taken great pains to educate the inhabitants of the island in the faith and principles of Christianity.

"They were in the uniform habit of morning and evening prayer and were regularly assembled on Sunday for religious instruction and worship. Books and paper of the *Bounty* furnished them with the means of considerable learning. Prayer books and a bible were among them, which were used in their devotions. It is probable also that Smith composed prayers and discourses particularly adapted to their circumstances. He had improved himself very much by reading and by the efforts he was obliged to make to instruct those under his care.

"The girls and boys were made to read and write before Captain Folger, to show him the degree of their improvement.

They did themselves great credit in both, particularly the girls! The journal of Smith was so handsomely kept so as to attract particular attraction and excite great regret that there was not time to copy it.

"When Smith was asked if he had heard of any great battles between the English and French fleets in the late wars, he answered, 'How could I, unless the birds of the air had been the heralds?' He was told of the victories of Lord Howe, Earl of St Vincent, Lord Duncan and Lord Nelson. He listened with attention till the narrative was finished and then rose from his seat, took off his hat, swung it around three times around his head with three cheers, threw it on the ground sailor like and cried out 'Old-England forever'. The young people around him appeared to be almost as much exhilarated as himself and must have looked on with no small surprise, having never seen their patriarchal chief so excited before.

"Smith was asked, if he should like to see his country again and particularly London, his native town. He answered, that he should, if he could return to his island, and his colony; but he had not the least desire to leave his present situation forever.

"The houses of this village were uncommonly neat. They were built after the manner of those at Otaheite. Small trees are felled and cut into suitable lengths; they are driven into the earth and are interwoven with bamboo; they are thatched with the leaves of the plantain and cocoa-nut... My impression is that Folger told me some of them were built of stone."

John Adams

JOHN ADAMS'S HOUSE.

Lithograph of John Adam's house in 1860.

"The young men labored in the fields and gardens and were employed in the several kinds of manufactures required by their situation. The girls made cloth from the cloth tree and attended to their domestic concerns. They had several amusements, dancing, jumping, hopping, running and various feats of activity. They were as cheerful as industrious, and healthy and beautiful as they were temperate and simple. They were obliged to cultivate their land with just spade and hoe." Captain Beatty, a later visitor, described the girls' appearances as 'Spanish'.

"The provision set before Captain Folger consisted of fowls, pork, and vegetables, cooked with great neatness and uncommonly well. The fruits also were excellent. The apron and shawl worn by the girls were made from the bark of the cloth tree. This is taken off the trunk, not longitudinally, but round. It is beaten till it is thin and soft and fit for use. The natural colour is buff, but it is dyed variously red, blue, and black and is covered with the figures of animals, birds and fish."

Delano continued, "The inquiry was made of Smith very particularly in regard to the conduct of the sexes toward each other, and the answer was given in such a manner as entirely to satisfy Captain Folger that the purest morals had thus far prevailed among them. Whatever might be the liberties allowed by the few original Otaheitan women remaining, the young people were remarkably obedient to the laws of continence, which had been taught them by their common instructor and guide."

Smith is said, by later visitors, to have changed his name to John Adams. This probably arose from a political conversation between him and Captain Folger, and from the account then given to Smith of the *Pandora* under the command of Captain Edwards, who was sent out in pursuit of the *Bounty* and the mutineers. "The fears of Smith were somewhat excited by this last article of intelligence." Captain Folger had given Smith an enthusiastic account of the new American government, including the distinguished President John Adams.

It was in fact an extraordinary coincidence that Smith's real name actually was also John Adams. He came from the back streets of London and signed up as Alexander Smith, an 'able seaman' – for the *Bounty* voyage. This was common for sailors wanting to lie low.

Much has been made of the social cocktail of these migrants in Pitcairn's Island. It mixed cultures, race, sex, power and violence with a backcloth of isolation, mutiny and treachery. The mutineers suffered their own mutiny from their native 'servants'. Subsequently, native killed native and white man killed white man and finally the Polynesian women slaughtered their Polynesian men. Smith deserves credit in saving this colony.

"When Folger was about to leave the island, the people pressed 'round him with the warmest affection and courtesy. The chronometer (K2) which was given him, although made of gold, was so black with smoke and dust that the metal could not be discovered. The girls brought some presents of cloth, which they made with their own hands and which they had dyed with beautiful colours. Their unaffected and amiable manners and their earnest prayers for his welfare, made a deep impression upon his mind and they are still cherished in his memory. He wished to decline taking all that was brought him in the overflow of friendship, but Smith told him it would hurt the feelings of the donors and the gifts could well be spared from the island. Folger made as suitable a return of presents as his ship afforded and left this most interesting community with the keenest sensations of regret. It reminded him of Paradise."

Mary Folger later wrote to a friend in 1846 after she was widowed, quoting her husband about the exchange of presents and departure: "After leaving the island he proceeded on his voyage in pursuit of seals..."[148] Samuel and Amy Coates, Quaker friends of Mayhew Folger, quoted in an undated letter a conversation in Philadelphia with Mayhew: "On parting we exchanged a few presents – Alec gave me the Chronometer & Compasse(s) of Bligh's Ship & some provisions & I gave him a few Article & we parted not without tears." Captain Folger had K2 in his hands.

K2 ON PITCAIRN: At last, the mystery of the *Bounty* mutineers had been solved and the missing 2nd Kendall chronometer had been found. 'Chronometer' was now in common usage. This unique navigational tool had been made in Britain and was now being passed from British hands to friendly American hands. Folger was anxious to reciprocate with a present and handed Alec a silk handkerchief which much pleased him. Folger was also presented with the Bounty's Azimuth Compass and a beautiful China porcelain bowl – the 'Pitcairn Porcelain' at the same time. These items also had their own stories to tell.

Nordoff and Hall, in their 1934 trilogy about the *Bounty* saga, set out to tell the whole story in a style appropriate to popular reading. Their books are a mixture of well researched fact and imaginative fiction, partly pieced together from additional information imparted by John Adams and a range of post-Folger visitors.[149] Nordoff and Hall indicated that Fletcher Christian, the only officer, took personal charge of all the navigation instruments in Pitcairn, which is totally believable.

Christian must have spent countless hours staring at K2 on his table when attending the daily clockwork winding, which told him the time in Greenwich. The technology. The shiny silver case. The 3 clock dials within one case. Hours. Minutes.

---

[148] Mary Folger to Mary Rappee, respected friend , 7 Month 18 1848
[149] Pitcairn's Island, Nordoff & Hall 1934. Info from Captain Folger, Capt Staines & Capt Pipon, 1814; Capt Beechey, 1825; Moerenhout, 1829; Walter Brodie, 1850; and other sources

Seconds. The 3 hands all moving at different speeds. The repetitive ticking. He must have endlessly read 'LARCUM KENDALL' with 'LONDON' under the name while sitting alone, staring in the stillness of the night. A thousand nights but with only one story.

Nordoff and Hall would 'quote' Smith. They referred to Christian's two-storey house, where one room on the lower floor was reserved for his use. "A roughly fashioned chair stood by a table of oak which held a silver-clasped Bible and a Book of Common Prayer, the *Bounty's* azimuth compass, and a fine timekeeper by Kendall of London. Christian wound the instrument daily and checked it from time to time by means of lunar observations, taken with the help of Young."[150]

There is reference to Smith sitting at Christian's table: "The two men were silent for a time while the chronometer beside them ticked loudly and steadily. Christian glanced at its dial, which registered the hour in Greenwich and set his thoughts wandering back through the past."

"Had that old timekeeper a voice,' Christian remarked, "it could tell us a rare tale! It was Captain Cook's shipmate on two voyages, travelling thousands of leagues over seas little known even now. It began life in London and it will end its days on Pitcairn's Island."[151]

This paragraph may be the source of the myth that the *Bounty* chronometer K2 was used by Captain Cook, when in fact he had sailed with K1 and also with K3 on his 3rd and last voyage.

Nordoff and Hall purport that after the uprisings, Aleck was deemed to have claimed the *Bounty's* chronometer from Christian's House. "Fletcher had kept it going from the time the ship was seized from Captain Bligh to the day he was killed. Mr. Young minded it after that, till he took to drinking so hard; then I'd looked after it. Anyway, I never missed a day in winding it and I took charge of Mr. Christian's calendar."[152] The tarnished condition of K2 when Folger received it, undermines this boast.

[150] Ibid, p92
[151] Ibid, p106
[152] Ibid, p265 (3071 words) 05.07.17

Every day, Fletcher Christian thought of Greenwich.

The *Topaz* log book included the information that "all the children of the deceased mutineers Speak tolerable English, some of them have grown to the Size of men & women, and to do them justice I think them a very human & hospitable people, and whatever may have Been the Errors or Crimes of Smith the Mutineer in times Back he is at present in my Opinion a worthy man and may be useful to Navigators who traverse this immense ocean. Such is the history of Christian & his associates be it remembered that this Island is Scantily Supplied with water So that it is impossible for a ship to Get a Supply. I place it in Lat 25° South, and 130° West Lon. from my last Lunar observations."

DEPARTURE: It was seal hunting time. The exchange of presents was over. *Topaz* Log Book, Sunday, 7 February: "Light airs from the Eastward & very hot the Ship Laying off & on. I tarried on shore with the Friendly Smith and his truly good people until 4 pm then left them and went on b'd and made Sail steering S E & S E B E Bound for Massafuro having rec'd from the people onshore some hogs, cocoa nuts and Plantains, at noon the Isle Bore N W B N by Compass 34' dis Lat'd Obsn 25° 11' S Lon by acct 129° 41' W."

Captain Folger sailed on with K2, a *Bounty* compass and the exquisite Chinese Pitcairn Porcelain into Spanish waters.

> Pitcairn dark in the sunset,
> Lone in a lonely sea,
> Islander race arising,
> Born of the wild and free,
> Cometh across the water,
> Sound of their song afar,
> Soft in the distance dying,
> Pitcairn from Panama.

Verse from poem 'The Track' by Lady Gwendolen Game, 1934, wife of governor of NSW.

Chapter 14
Captain Folger in Spanish Waters
Vengencia Espanola
1808 K2: 6th and 7th Voyages

Captain Folger said to a Quaker friend Samuel Coates years later, that on leaving Pitcairn, "they parted not without tears". Despite these tears, Mayhew Folger couldn't stay at Pitcairn any longer without anchorage. His boat was manned by his crew for his few hours on this secretive island and he was well behind on his hunting schedule. The only way he could rectify this was to search for seals. Find them. Kill them. Skin them. He had been successful eight years earlier in 1800 in his seal hunt at Mas Afuera and must have been confident he would succeed again in these islands.

It took another month to reach his destination and he had time to reminisce on his dramatic discovery at Pitcairn and to ponder on his gifts and exchanges with the islanders. His prime acquisition must have been the K2 Bounty Watch which he was taking on its 6th voyage.

As he honed and polished the casing, his heart must have been thumping with rising excitement when the shine gradually turned to a glittering gold. This is how Amasa Delano later described the casing of K2 and he could only have obtained that information from Folger.[153] "The chronometer…though of gold, was so black with smoke & dust that the metal could not be discovered."

The Azimuth Compass was a new addition to Folger's range of navigational instruments at his disposal on this voyage. It was

---

[153] Delano, Narrative, p143

built with a sight to take bearings on the horizon including specific points on shore.

Arriving at Mas Afuera on 15 March 1808, Folger must have been distraught by the lack of seals. By then, it was the wrong time of the year and the well-known prime killing fields were devastated by competing international sealers. Folgers decided to land at Juan Fernandez to buy fresh food for his crew.

Being aware that Spanish colonies did not welcome American and British vessels and were prone to some enterprising piracy, Folger sent a letter to the Governor on 20 March, requesting permission to land, bring the sick ashore and buy provisions. Two days later the Governor agreed and invited the Captain to his house. It was too good to be true!

A subsequent letter from Folger to his employers, Boardman & Pope in Boston dated 10 September 1808, [154]describes his story well: "They Fired Eight 24-pounders at her (*Topaz*), wounded our Rigging and Fore top mast, took all hands on Shore and put them in Prison and commenced robbing the Ship of everything they thought proper to take away."

The letter continues, "They took all the Clothes on Shore, so that before night there was scarcely one among us all that had a change of clothing. The Governor then declared that I was a Prisoner of War... I was kept on shore and the chief Mate with one other was kept on Board under a Guard."

This continued until the 14 April 1808, "...then arrived a Spanish ship from the Continent (of S. America) with a New Governor. By this time, everything of consequence was taken; bread and salt and provisions excepted – even our Boat Anchors & Sealing Clubs were taken away"[155].

Vengencia Espanola. This '*Topaz*' episode is regularly described as "Spanish Piracy" and "Spanish Perfidy", although the islanders themselves would have felt it was justified "Spanish Vengeance". They believed they had all rights in these 'Spanish' islands and waters.

The Spanish with their historic fleets and galleons laden with New World treasures, had for hundreds of years suffered from

---

[154] E Stackpole, Sea Hunters, p240
[155] Ibid

worldwide piracy, so they were prone to take their own opportunities. International whaling and seal hunting was frequently carried out on Spanish land and waters. Even in 1808, the Spanish could point to the islands around Juan Fernandez to prove the devastation of their seal colonies.

In 1807, the Spanish were allies of Napoleon when he invaded Portugal. However, in early 1808, Napoleon decided to take over Spain as well, which then forced a new unusual alliance of Spain, Britain and Portugal against France. The new French threat to the Portuguese royal family led to its evacuation to Brazil, closely escorted by the Royal Navy. The Iberian Peninsula wars were commanded by Wellington for the allies, backed up with extensive guerrilla tactics by Spanish patriots, determined to take their own 'Vengencia Espanola' on France.

In 1808, America was not at war with Spain. However, Folger spoke English. That was a good enough reason for this act of piracy. Furthermore, the Spanish would be aware that the Americans by this time were probably the most active seal hunters in the Pacific. The Spanish not only took the 600 seal skins but even the sealing clubs from the *Topaz*.

The *Topaz* was held in Juan Fernandez until 22 April 1808, when the new Governor ordered Folger and his crew to be released so they could be escorted by the military and their armed ship *Castor* to Valparaiso, so that another search of the *Topaz* could be carried out by the mainland authorities. K2 was now under Spanish control and it was being taken on its 7th voyage to the South American mainland under Spanish guard.

Once on the mainland, Folger and the crew were free to move about but were initially refused access to the *Topaz*. After some time, the inspectors confirmed the boat was not suspicious and gave Folger a certificate.

Frustrating months followed as Folger used his certificate to claim compensation. Even finding the right person with power was an achievement. Various locals gave advice suggesting a visit to the Viceroy in Lima, Peru or the capital in Santiago.[156] His letter to Boardman & Pope shows his frustration: "Whether I ever shall get anything, is uncertain, for they seem to have no idea of Justice in this country... If I fail, I can see no other

---

[156] Walter Hayes, The Captain from Nantucket, p43

prospect at present but that of selling the Ship, as my people are nearly naked."

While in Santiago, Folger was given clearance papers for himself, his crew and his Ship on July 22, 1808. However, his hopes for actual financial compensation for the thefts from the *Topaz* looked dim. At this time, motherland Spain had begun a 'war of national liberation' against France. The colonial based Spanish authorities probably had higher priorities than compensating foreign seal hunters.

Much of this experience is poignantly covered in a rarely published letter from Mayhew Folger to his beloved wife Mary Joy Folger who was still anxiously waiting in Nantucket. She had heard nothing from him for nearly two years:

"Valparaiso, 29 March 1809"[157]

"My dear wife,

When I heard last by the way of Buenos Ayres, I was in great hopes of getting redress for loss of Property and time in this country and after a long lawsuit with this government and having one Sentence in my favour, my ship's papers were on the 13th of January deliver'd to me and I order'd to repair immediately to Valparaiso and proceed to sea, and the favourage sentence which expressed that I was to receive upwards of Fourty four thousand Dollars was put aside , I then call'd for a copy of their proceedings which was refused, and to proceed on my voyage without a supply of money to procure necessaries which I had been robbed of, was impossible.

I then petitioned for License to sell the ship which was also refused, at the same time an order was issued for me to Leave the Capital in 24 hours, which I thought proper to Obey having a promise at the same time that I should receive a copy of the Proceedings of the Court when I was about to embark.

I accordingly set out for this place where I arrived on the 21st Jan. had a survey of the Ship and the Surveyors reports that she was unable to proceed on the voyage without very considerable supplies. At the same time my creditors call'd on me for debts I had contracted, for the Support of myself and Ship's Company, in consequence of which I was obliged to sell

---

[157] Nantucket Historical Association

articles that i could best spare, the principle of which was Rum, they deducting 44 per cent on the sales by way of duties.

I have at length got through with this sale and satisfied my creditors from which it may well be that my dents were not enormous. The Government have also sent me such papers as they thought proper to send, but very far from being a copy of the Proceedings, ashamed I presume that their proceedings should be made public, but such as they are I must proceed with to Lima, there Protest and pray for permission to take a Freight for Old Spain or sell the Ship. I am now waiting only for the post to arrive from Santiago to gain some intelligence which will be necessary on my arrival in Lima.

When I was taken I had on board 44 men and Boys, twenty-one of them have deserted but I have enough left to navigate around the Globe, but there I have left as well as those who deserted and are in want of every kind of Clothing, and I am quite unable to supply them of myself. Thus have I been harassed for these twelve months past – far, very far, the most unpleasant year of my Life, yet I never knew one to pass so swiftly.

If I can get a freight from Lima to Spain the voyage may not end so...(unclear) even if I could have...(unclear) there would have been no loss on the voyage, and my chief study must be to find which way I can move to lose the least, for gaining is entirely out of the Question, if I cannot get a freight in Lima I am in hopes some way or the other to bring to a crisis a voyage every way replete with adversity.

Nearly two years have elapsed since we parted, during that time I have never heard one word from thee, but hope in Lima to be able to collect some news, and also to forward Letters home for I have lately rec'd information that some of the Letters I've sent have been interrupted and very possibly they all have.

I remain my dear Wife
With the truest esteem
Thy affectionate Husband

Mayhew Folger"

This is a fascinating historical letter. The Folgers' marriage was a love match. They had no contact for nearly two years. Yet, his letter asks nothing about Mary Joy's welfare; or of his beloved children, or of his extensive family, or their community of Friends. The only personal remarks were in the salutations 'my dear wife' and he had never heard 'a word from thee'. The vast majority of his letter was an obsessive detailed narrative of his own problems. This surely indicates intense frustration and stress.

When Folger finally took back his ship he must have bitterly regretted polishing up the K2-timekeeper to look like gold. Not surprisingly, K2 was gone. Strangely enough, the Bounty Azimuth Compass was still on the ship. Perhaps it looked scruffy enough to be deemed valueless? Perhaps more important, they overlooked the Chinese made Pitcairn Porcelain.

The Royal Navy was given responsibility to bring over the Portuguese Royal family and government in 1807 to Brazil for protection from Napoleon. The fleet sailing across the Atlantic, included most of the Portuguese navy, as well as a covering screen of British warships. Rear Admiral Sir Sydney Smith commanded it from the *Foudroyant*, a major 74-gunner. A welcoming Rio de Janeiro became a Royal Navy station.

It was not only American sailors who had problems with Spanish authorities in Chile and there were significant numbers of British sailors either in prison or destitute. Sir Sydney Smith despatched an enterprising lieutenant called William Fitzmaurice in two sloops to Valparaiso carrying diplomatic letters requesting the release of such mariners. By mid-1808, Britain was a military ally of Spain and also needed all the sailors it could find.

Folger and Fitzmaurice were both in Valparaiso at the same time and arranged a meeting on the 10 October 2008. Folger attended the meeting with his second mate and his log book. Folger clearly succeeded in convincing Fitzmaurice of their story, since the lieutenant took the trouble to copy a complete page from the *Topaz* log book. Folger related the whole story about the *Bounty* mutineers, the K2-chronometer and the azimuth compass to an astonished Fitzmaurice.

Lieutenant William Fitzmaurice then sent a two page report to Admiral Sir Sydney Smith who in turn forwarded it five months later to the Admiralty in London.[158]

---

[158] PRO ADM 1/19

HMS Foudroyant
at Sea, 14th March 1809
Lat 27° 37' Longd 29° 30'W

"Sir, I take a safe opportunity of sending an extract from the Log of the American Ship Topaz of Boston, giving a more precise account of the fate of the Bounty, Christian and other mutineers who remained in her after quitting Otaheite (Tahiti) than I believe is known at the Admiralty. It is certified by Lieut. Fitzmaurice.

I have the honour to be sir
Your most obedient humble servant
W. Sydney Smith."

The report was handwritten by Fitzmaurice and sent by Sydney Smith to William Wellesley Pole, Secretary of the Naval Office. This Fitzmaurice report includes:

Valparaiso, 10 Oct 1808

Extract from Log Book of Captain Folger of the American ship *Topaz* of Boston.

"Folger related upon landing upon Pitcairn's Island (or Incanation to Quiros) in Lat 25° 02' Longd 130° 00'W (by lunar Obsn) he found there an Englishman by the name of Alexr Smith, the only person remaining of Nine that escaped in His Majesty's late ship *Bounty*, Capt Bligh in the Boat, Christian the leader of the mutiny, took command of the Ship and went to Otaheite where great part of the crew left the ship except himself, Smith and seven others who each took wives and six Otaheitan Men as Servants & shortly after arrived at this island (Pitcairn) where they run the Ship on Shore and broke her up; this event taking place in 1790.

"About 4 years after their Arrival (a great jealousy existing) the Otaheitans secretly revolted & killed every Englishmen except himself, who they severely wounded in the neck with a pistol ball. The same night the widows of the deceased Englishmen arose and put to death the whole of the Otaheitans, leaving Smith the only Man alive upon the Island with 8 or 9 women and several small children…

"The 2nd Mate of the *Topaz* asserts that Christian the ring leader became Insane & shortly after their Arrival on the Island, threw himself off the Rocks into the Sea, another died of a Fever before the Massacre of the whole took place…the whole population amounts to about 33 who acknowledge Smith as Father and commander of them all, they all speak English and have been educated by him; Captain Folger represents – in a religious and moral way.

"The Island is badly supplied with Water sufficient only for the present inhabitants & no anchorage. Smith gave to Capt. Folger a Chronometer made by Kendall which was taken from him by the Govr of Juan Fernandez."

Extracted from the *Topaz* Log Book, 20 Sept 1808. Wm. Fitzmaurice

These two letters, eventually, arrived at the British Admiralty on 14 May 1809. This was the first news of Fletcher Christian's group of mutineers to reach London. Bearing in mind that over 20 years had passed and Britain and its allies were locked in a 'war to the finish' with Napoleon, there was little response from the Admiralty.

Copies were taken and Folger's letter passed to the Times Newspaper for the 1 July 1809 edition, the Naval Review and Quarterly Review.

These publications were largely written for the establishment and included this outrageous comment: "If this interesting relation rested solely on the faith that is due to Americans, with whom we say with regret, truth is not always considered a moral obligation, we should hesitate giving it this publicity… two facts on the credibility of the story on which they must stand or fall are 'the name of the mutineer and the maker of the time-piece'."

The Quarterly Review carried out some research and concluded that an Alexander Smith appears in the books of the *Bounty* as follows: "Entered 7 Sep. 1787 Ab. Born in London. Aged 20. Run 28 April 1789. One of the mutineers. It appears that the *Bounty* was actually supplied with a time-piece by Kendall."

Despite the advice from Folger about the inaccuracy of Captain Carteret's location for Pitcairn's Island, the Carteret location stayed on naval and commercial maps for years.

By this time, the Spanish authorities in Chile had given sufficient compensation to Captain Folger to take his ship and crew and leave their shores. However, Folger was desperate to bring something back home to his employers, to justify this extended trip.

"At Guayaquil, he found merchants with copper, cocoa and Peruvian bark destined for Spain and with six Spanish Dons as passengers he sailed from Lima on January 2 1810 for Cadiz."[159] He later met a British captain who informed him that all Spain except Cadiz was in French hands.

Folger needed another destination so he headed to Boston where he arrived on 27 May 1810, where he arranged the sale of his passenger's cargo and also made a handsome profit for himself. A historic voyage – lasting 3 years and 51 days.

Captain Mayhew Folger of Nantucket, never went to sea again. K2 – The Bounty Watch – stayed in Spanish hands for over 30 years.

---

[159] Walter Hayes, The Captain from Nantucket, p79

Chapter 15
Bounty Compass Returns
1812-14 War

The loss of the K2 Bounty Watch was a major blow to Captain Folger, but there was some consolation for a mariner by still having the *Bounty* Azimuth Compass, which Alex Smith had also given him before leaving Pitcairn. The Spanish officials overlooked this navigational instrument. On this last step of the voyage, he had more time to study the instrument, clean it and even use it.

He confirmed in a later personal letter to the British Admiralty that he had not only actually used it at sea, but had also upgraded it in Boston.

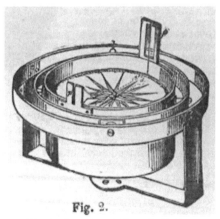

Fig. 2.

Example of an Azimuth Compass.

One can only imagine Captain Folger's feelings, sailing past his home town of Nantucket as he made his way back to Boston harbour after more than three years. How was his wife? His children? His extended Quaker family? His home? His prospects? Fortune smiled on him in this last part of his voyage. Although he turned his faithful ship *Topaz* away from French occupied Spain, he brought sufficient goods back from South America to produce a profit for him and his employer Boardman & Pope.

Folger's whole family must have been overjoyed to see him. The absence must have been hardest on his wife, who had to manage a growing family. There would be inevitable contention about Mayhew going to sea again after such a long voyage. Mayhew had 'salt water' in his veins but was a devoted family man who still had to earn a living.

Even in 1809 and 1810 there was the smell of war in the air. British cruisers were stopping American ships on the high seas searching for deserters. When cornered, it was common for British deserters to throw themselves into the sea, rather than face Royal Navy justice.

All this was particularly bad news for the fishermen, whalers and sealers of Nantucket, Boston and New Bedford. They had seen it all before in the War of Independence when their fishing and seal hunting industry was destroyed. Their largely Quaker upbringing meant they deplored war – and wanted to stay neutral. The Friends started leaving Nantucket even before President Madison declared war on Britain in 1812.

Once the war started, the bulk of American commercial shipping was blockaded by both warships and privateers. There were some dramatic American successes with the brilliantly designed large 'super frigates', but even that couldn't stop the tight stranglehold of this naval blockade. A prominent Quaker, Obed Macy wrote in his 'Diary' that: "British cruisers were so numerous on the coast as to render it very hazardous for the coasters to pass which had usually supplied the market with bread stuffs."[160]

The 'pull' on the Folger family to move as more Friends and relations settled inland had its due effect. Mayhew's sister was married to a member of the Coffin family who were prominent, wealthy residents in Philadelphia, so she and their three children

---

[160] Nantucket Historical Association and Sea Hunters, p260

moved in with them, while Mayhew continued sorting out his affairs.

While in Philadelphia, Mayhew Folger met up with neighbours Samuel Coates and his wife. Samuel Coates, who was a respected business man and charity supporter, was intrigued with Captain Folger's adventurous story so carefully wrote it down. The copy largely covers the same ground as earlier transcriptions but was a particularly full version. This copy appeared undated but was probably transcribed between 1811 and 1813.

It started with "I was at Pitcairn's, on the Pacific Ocean" (Feb 7, 1808). It interestingly ended with "on parting we exchanged a few presents – Alec gave me the Chronometer and Compass of Bligh's Ship and some provisions & I gave him a few articles & we parted not without tears". This particular record by Samuel Coates confirmed that Folger was consistent with his story.[161]

Folger's relation Thomas Coffin decided to move to Ohio. There appeared to be better prospects and more land available. So in August 1813, the Folgers took the plunge and moved westwards to a small town called Kendal. It seems an amazing coincidence that having rediscovered the *Bounty* mutineers and the lost K2 Kendall chronometer, that Captain Mayhew Folger should end his days in Kendal, Ohio.

Several months before leaving Philadelphia, Mayhew would have gone back to Nantucket to pack up and decide what to take with him and what to leave behind. Folger had received no thanks or comment from the British Admiralty following the transcription of the Pitcairn discovery taken by Lieutenant Fitzmaurice in Valparaiso. He was probably confident that the young British naval officer would have forwarded his report to Sir Sydney Smith but Folger heard nothing.

Although Folger no longer had the Bounty Watch, he did still have in his possession the 'Bounty Azimuth Compass'. Legally, this was still British property and he seems to have decided that despite the War of 1812, the British Admiralty should have it back. It was a good opportunity for Folger to send his own

---

[161] Walter Hayes, The Captain from Nantucket, p95

personal letter direct, instead of relying on other people's versions.

The first task was to write a letter and decide who to address it to. The second task was working out how to deliver the letter and azimuth compass during a war. A second letter was then addressed to a friendly merchant who worked for a trading company called Borden Chase in New York that appeared to have international contacts.

New York, 4 April 1813[162]
TO: Esteem'd Friend
Borden Chase

"I have order'd to be left at your Store a Compass which I wish you to forward to England by first oppy (opportunity) – with a letter directed to the Right Honourable Lords of the Admiralty – Perhaps by applying to Col. Barclay Agent for British prisoners he could put you in a way to forward it. The circumstances attending this compass makes me anxious to have it forwarded as early as possible. On my last voyage to the Pacific Ocean in 1808... (brief description of finding Pitcairn) he (Alex Smith) presented me with a timekeeper and azimuth compass which belonged to his Britannic Majesty's Ship Bounty. The timekeeper was taken from me about 6 weeks afterwards...the compass I brought home with me which is the one above mentioned and will perhaps be worth their Lordships acceptance merely from the circumstances attending it."

I Remain Respectfully
your etc etc
Mayhew Folger

Possibly because of the war, Borden Chase took a long time to arrange a delivery. They understandably waited until an end to hostilities looked imminent. The peace treaty was struck on Christmas Eve 1814 in Belgium but actual delivery of the azimuth compass into British hands in America happened within days – 5 January 1815. Since America wouldn't hear about the

---

[162] UK – PRO ADM 1/508

Treaty of Ghent for at least a month, the transaction effectively took place during the war.

Peace was sealed in Belgium with a handshake between James Gambier, Admiral of the Fleet, with Ambassador John Quincy Adams. This multilingual American politician and diplomat would later become the 6th President of the United States. Surely, there's no family connection between the President and mutineer John Adams on Pitcairn, who hid under the name of Smith?

The contact for the physical transfer of this parcel from Nantucket was Rear Admiral Sir Henry Hotham on HMS *Superb* sailing near New London, who then addressed it to the British Admiralty as follows:

John Wilson Croker Esqr,
Secretary to the Admiralty.

Sir, The enclosed letter addressed to the Lords Commissioners of the Admiralty; (accompanied by an Azimuth Compass of His Majesty's late ship Bounty) stating the fate of several of the Mutineers of that Ship etc having been delivered to me by an inhabitant of the island of Nantucket, with a request that they might be sent to their Lordships; I do myself the honour to forward them to you.

> *I have the honour to be Sir,*
> *Your most obedient humble Servant*
> *Henry Hotham, Rear Admiral.*

The parcel from Nantucket contained both the 'Bounty Azimuth Compass' and Captain Folger's flowery and courteous letter. It appears to be the only one ever written by Captain Mayhew Folger directly to the British Admiralty.
"Right Honourable Lords of the Admiralty".
Nantucket, 1 March 1813.
"My Lords,

The remarkable circumstances which took place on my last voyage to the Pacific Ocean, will I trust plead my apology for addressing your Lordships at this time. In Febr. 1808 I touched at Pitcairn's Island in Lat 25° 2' South – Lon 130° West from Greenwich – my principal object was to procure Seal skins for the China Market – and from the account given in Capt Carterets voyage – I supposed the Island was uninhabited – but on approaching the shore in my boat, I was met by three young men in a double Canoe with a present, consisting of some fruit and a hog, they spoke to me in the English Language, and inform'd me they were born on the island and their father was an Englishman, by the name of Alexander Smith who inform'd me he was one of the Bounty's Crew, and after putting Capt Bligh on the boat with half the ship's company they returned to Otaheite, where part of their Crew chose to tarry – but Mr. Christian with eight others including himself prefer'd going to a more remote place, and after – making a short stay at Otaheite, where they took wives and six man servants, they proceeded to Pitcairn's where they destroy'd the Ship.

After taking everything out of her which they thought would be useful to them... About six years after they landed at this place, their servants attacked and killed all the English except my informant, & he was severely wounded – the same night the Otaheitan widows arose & murder'd all their Countrymen, leaving Smith with the widows & children where he had resided ever since without being visited.

I remained but a short time on the Island & on leaving it, Smith presented me a Timekeeper (K2) and an azimuth compass, which he told me belonged to the Bounty; the Timekeeper was taken from me by the Governor of the Island of Juan Fernandez after I had it in my possession about six weeks – the compass I put in repair on board my ship and made use of it on my homeward passage, since when a new Card has been put in by an instrument maker in Boston.

I now forward it to your Lordships – thinking there will be some satisfaction in receiving it merely from the extraordinary circumstances attending... Should you wish any further information respecting Pitcairns Island or its inhabitants – a letter directed to me at Nantucket to the care of Gideon Gardner Esqr will be carefully attended.

I am your Lords
your Lordships most Obedt.
and very humble Servant
Mayhew Folger."[163]

The letter and compass were received in London on 25 February 1815. There were instructions to "write to Mr. Folger and thank him for his letter"[164]. Folger's letter of 1 March 1813, made no mention of his earlier communication via Lieutenant Fitzmaurice when in Valparaiso in 1808, which was received by the Admiralty on 14 May 1809.

Although the British frigates *Briton* and *Tagus* under Captains Staines and Pipon had, meanwhile, visited Pitcairn, they didn't return to England with this news until some months after Captain Folger's personal letter with the *Bounty* Azimuth Compass had already arrived at the Admiralty in London.

K2 and the azimuth compass were not the only gifts exchanged between Folger and 'Alec Smith'. The Pitcairn Porcelain was also handed over to Folger. It is a small Chinese bowl, probably part of a set that had been given to Fletcher Christian by his family. It is hand-painted with a wonderful design of peonies and golden pheasants. It's fortunate that the Spanish didn't take it as well as the chronometer. The one bowl is displayed at the NHA in Nantucket.

No longer an active captain, Mayhew Folger remained with his family in Kendal, Ohio where he bought land at a good price, built a saw mill and kept involved in local affairs.[165] Folger kept in touch with local sea captains and his old friend Amasa Delano whom he met again in Boston after 1810 and from whom he received a letter at his Kendal address dated 16 June 1816.

Delano was just seeking any further snippets for his 1817 'Narrative' but Folger could only really confirm some of his earlier reports and that he would be "pleased to see his work" and that "it must be very interesting".[166] Folger came to Kendal before he was forty but unfortunately died young at forty-four on

---

[163] Ibid
[164] Ibid (2) above p85
[165] W Hayes, The Captain, p88
[166] Delano Voyages, 1817, Ch.v

1 September 1828. Mary Joy was blessed with a large family and Friends and lived a full life until she died aged 81.

Folger's Pitcairn adventure remained a favourite family story and Mary Joy wrote an interesting and rarely published letter from Richmond on 18 July 1846 to a friend, Mary Rappie, in Canton, Ohio.

Respected Friend,
Mary Rappie (1st para): "Having heard thou wishes to learn something of the particulars of my husband's discovery of Pitcairn's Island in 1807; I have penned some of the facts as I recollect them, hoping they may interest thee."
(2nd para): *"He left Boston in the ship Topaz on a sealing voyage..."*

The rest of Mary's clearly written letter covered the story as consistently as her husband, when recollecting his voyage. A particularly interesting paragraph is: "Smith gave him a chronometer worth six hundred dollars and an azimuth compass."[167]

Since new chronometers from 1810 could be purchased for a fraction of six hundred dollars and K2 had no real antiquity value at that time, this written valuation re-enforces Amasa Delano's report in his Narrative in 1817 that Mayhew Folger believed that K2 was probably made of 'gold'. He may well have gone to his grave with that belief.

---

[167] Nantucket Historical Assoc.
Images: P15a. Public domain

Chapter 16
K2 by Mule – The Andes
K2 8th Voyage
Captain Herbert in China Opium Wars
1840 K2 9th Voyage

19 February 1840, HMS *Calliope* sailed into Valparaiso harbour, Chile. It had left Spithead in England in mid-August 1839 under Captain Thomas Herbert and headed to Jamaica before going on to Brazil and Montevideo. The task along the east coast of South America was in essence, showing the flag in troubled regions, protecting British interests and keeping a close eye on the French fleet, which was active in the River Plate.

Once the *Calliope* was released from these duties, the crew sailed the ship around Cape Horn and worked their way along the west coast of South America to Valparaiso, the current RN base for Pacific operations. They would relax, take on victuals, carry out any works and receive their new naval orders.

HMS *Calliope* was a 28-gun 6th rate frigate, which was launched in mid-1837 in the Sheerness dockyard but had not yet been blooded in war. By then, the usage of the 'HMS' prefix before Royal Navy ship's names, had become standard.

Captain Herbert was 47, born in County Kerry and volunteered to join the Royal Navy as a midshipman. From just 21 years of age, he had a very successful career capturing five privateers in the West Indies and performed well in the War of 1812–1814. He had been active in the Potomac River which led to the capture of Fort Washington.

Sir Thomas Herbert

Once in Valparaiso, Captain Herbert was contacted by Alexander Caldcleugh, a British expatriate who brought to him an amazing story and a proposition. He mainly lived in Santiago, owned copper mines, held financial posts and had travelled widely in South America.

Caldcleugh was a friend of Charles Darwin who had spent part of 1834 to 1835 away from his ship *Beagle,* while carrying out his own expeditions with his assistant Sym Covington exploring the geology, animals, plants, fish and insects of this region.

Darwin must have been thrilled to meet Caldcleugh since Darwin had read his 'Travels in South America 1825' while he was still at Oxford. Darwin stayed in Santiago with Caldcleugh, who gave him advice about the terrain, routes and history of the country. Darwin wrote in his diaries that his new friend went to "an infinite degree of trouble for me".

They were both members of the Royal Society with Caldcleugh becoming a fellow in 1831 while Darwin's fellowship came later in 1839. Both were scientists and it is highly likely that they discussed chronometers, since the *Beagle* sailed with twenty two of them on board.

Caldcleugh showed Captain Herbert a large watch as wide as his hand. The casing was tarnished as if it hadn't been polished or cleaned for decades. Herbert would have recognised that this heavy object must be some sort of marine watch. The dial of the watch included the words 'Larcum Kendall' and 'London'.

This clearly identified it as one of the three Kendall maritime watches. This timekeeper had disappeared over 50 years ago when K2 was assigned to the *Bounty* and then confiscated from Captain Folger by Spanish officials in 1808. The loss of K2 in South America may have been fairly well known in England and America by then, so it was probably easy to identify it as the lost Bounty Watch.

The story told by Caldcleugh to Herbert was both exciting and almost unbelievable in that a local muleteer called Castillo had bought K2 in Concepcion for three doubloons and it had been in his family until he died in Santiago in 1840.[168]

How far had K2 travelled on the back of a mule? It is unclear whether it spent most of its time on a mule's back or under the new owner's mattress, but K2 appeared to have travelled to Valparaiso, Santiago and Concepcion. Depending on the routes over the Andes, this distance would probably be a couple of thousand kilometres 'as the mule plods'.

These distances would be quite a remarkable land voyage over the course of 30 years and arguably, was the 8th Voyage of K2.

Since Caldcleugh also lived in Santiago where Castillo died, his widow must have asked him to sell this large watch for her.

---

[168] Naval Chronicle 1840, p901

Her muleteer husband would probably have known it came off a ship, when he bought it. If the widow journeyed to Valparaiso on her own, she would not know who to approach. Caldcleugh was local to her, well known and could speak Spanish.

All that is known of the sale is that Herbert paid 50 guineas, which was probably comparable to a brand new marine chronometer in 1840. Whether Caldcleugh bought it from the widow or was acting as a commission agent, is still a mystery.[169]

Since K2 was understandably in poor shape, Captain Herbert was keen to restore it in both looks and working order, so on 18 May 1840 he took the chronometer to a local "watch and chronometer maker" called Mr Mouat, to "put in good order".[170] There was a race against time. Herbert was due to sail on 1 July, which only left 6 weeks to clean up K2 and get it working for him – to take back to England for presenting to The United Services Institution of London.

The back of the watch probably hadn't been opened for about 40 years. The last person to have seen inside K2 was likely to have been Young on Pitcairn's Island. Inside the watch, Mr Mouat found an engraved inscription:

Larcum Kendall
London
AD 1771

It must have been as a precaution that Captain Herbert approached Captain Newman who was also at Valparaiso with his sloop HMS *Sparrowhawk*, to handle a mission of taking K2 to London, if necessary. As it turned out, the repaired Kendall chronometer was delivered to Captain Herbert on HMS *Calliope* on 23 June, just one week before sailing.

When the *Calliope* departed on 1 July, K2 was on board on its last journey. Looking at all of the previous voyages of K2, one could consider this marine watch as being a jinx! If this last voyage was to be in another war zone, why not a war with China? The 9th voyage.

---

[169] 1 guinea is £1 + 1 shilling
[170] Naval Chronicle 1840, p904

While Herbert was joining a small fleet in the First Opium War against China with his precious K2 on board, Mr Mouat was still busy in Valparaiso. The clever Spanish watchmaker who brought K2 back to life, must have been in close consultation with Captain Newman who had been the 'back up' if the chronometer wasn't ready for Herbert. Although Herbert had K2, the documentation and diagrams were apparently not ready, so Captain Newman took over that particular responsibility.

Newman took detailed notes of the repairs – Mouat was impressed by K2 and "spoke in high terms of the beauty of the workmanship". The report was sent to Sir John Barrow who had always been fascinated by the *Bounty*/Pitcairn saga. Barrow was quick to go public with this news and sent a copy of Newman's document to the publishers of the 1840 Naval Chronicle.

Some points included in the document were "that the day 23 June it was delivered to him (Herbert) being fast on the Greenwich Mean Time and losing 3.5 seconds". Also, "once taken apart, it was in a Complete State of Preservation".

Newman continued, "the chronometer is not one of Kendall's copies of Harrison, the train being similar to that now being employed and the escapement that of the old or vertical kind." It was "Six inches in diameter with three dials on its face. The outer silver case is as they were 60–70 years ago with the appearance of a gigantic watch"[171].

Captain Newman added a personal postscript: "I was at Pitcairn's Island in the *Sparrowhawk* this time last year and perhaps that has contributed to the interest I feel in this affair. I have some tappa or native cloth manufactured by the hands of Polly Adams herself." Polly was, of course, the daughter of John Adams (alias Alex Smith) who had been the last mutineer on Pitcairn's Island, where he died in 1829.

Newman showed his officer corp breeding by declaring that this chronometer "is still legally the property of Her Majesty". Queen Victoria had started her long reign in 1837.

This report from Newman was dated 21 November 1840, Portsea, but possibly written while he was still at sea in HMS *Sparrowhawk*. There could be no actual presentations, until

---

[171] Ibid p901

Captain Herbert returned to Britain with the recovered and restored Bounty Watch.

Meanwhile, Captain Herbert in HMS *Calliope* was making a name for himself in the First Opium war with China, which lasted from 18 March 1839 to 29 August 1843. Britain had a great liking for Chinese silk, porcelain and tea but the Chinese really only wanted silver, which was effectively a currency.

Eventually, Britain and others found the perfect export product – opium. It was already being used for medical purposes in China but endless supplies from India rapidly built up a major addiction with Chinese customers at attractive profit levels for the East India Company.

Although initially tolerated by the Qing dynasty, the problem was getting out of hand so the Emperor appointed a commissioner called Lin to solve it. He tried to do this by confiscating 20,000 chests of opium in March 1839 without offering any compensation. Since Canton was the commercial centre, Lin also personally inspected the defences along the Pearl River.

The whole situation aroused extensive ethical debate back in Britain, but the war was technically started to claim compensation and to uphold 'the principle of free trade'.

When referring to the British flag in parliament in April 1840, Gladstone attacked Prime Minister Palmerston, "it has always been associated with the cause of justice, with the opposition to oppression, with respect for national rights, with honourable commercial enterprise, but now, under the auspices of the noble lord, that flag is hoisted to protect an infamous contraband trade".

Britain was not alone in this opportunity. France, and others, all wanted a slice of this rich cake.

Much of the fighting involved close operational cooperation between the army and the navy. An expeditionary force from Singapore including British and Indian troops fought their way towards Canton in June 1840, supported by a fleet including four steam-powered ships. The advanced technology in both army and navy combined with training and discipline, ensured British victories.

Attack on First Bar Canton River

The entrance to the Pearl River was defended by a number of forts so on 27 February 1841, a naval force of five frigates and two steamers attacked them. In command was Captain Thomas Herbert. The overall British fire power was devastating and the troops and marines had no problem in taking the forts, which ceased cannon fire within hours.

A government report states: "H.M. ships *Calliope, Larne* and *Hyacinth* under Captain Herbert proceeded to bombard the lower fort, while the steamer *Nemesis* and *Queen* threw shells into the hill fort and entrenchments."[172]

Herbert later reported: "I landed with some seamen and marines."

Over the next few months further forts were taken on the way to Canton. The Chinese navy consisted of a few East India ships but were mainly armed junks, which were no match against modern warships. Anti-piracy was a key reason for the Chinese navy and their government commented, "Cases of piracy are perpetually occurring, and even barbarian (western) barks anchor in our inner seas, without the least notice being taken of them'."[173]

---

[172] archive.org.narrative. Two years in China. Section 65
[173] Naval Chronicle, 1840, p275. Mouat – Chilean watch repairer: Naval Chronicle, 1840, Cambridge Library Coll, p901

'A Barbarian Sailor'
A Chinese view of a foreigner Sailor

On 14 June 1841, Captain Herbert got promoted to HMS *Blenheim* on the death of the current Captain Humphrey Fleming. Herbert moved from a 28-gun frigate to a major 74-gun, 3rd rate ship of the line, with a crew of 600. He immediately transferred to the *Blenheim* and took K2 with him.

Herbert was the senior naval officer on the Canton (Pearl) River and took part in further conquests by helping to capture Amoy, Chusan and finally Chinhai. Canton had been handed over with barely a shot and that opened up other opportunities. By mid-1842, the mouth of the Yangtze and the port Shanghai were also taken. The war was virtually over.

HMS *Blenheim*

The peace treaty of Nanking was signed on 29 August 1842 which included ceding Hong Kong to Britain, opening up 5 more ports for trading and millions of Pounds in compensation. This was the first 'unequal' treaty but more would follow in the Second Opium war of 1856-60.

Captain Herbert left the China war zone after the peace treaty, to sail back to Britain in HMS *Blenheim* via the Cape of Good Hope, which completed an 'around the world' voyage for him, after he landed on 28 March 1843. The ship was decommissioned at Sheerness in October 1843.

Herbert was returning home a hero and to many honours but he had also brought back K2, since he had long term plans for it.

Chapter 17
Greenwich
1963 K2 Returns

Captain Herbert received many honours on his return. One of his first plans was to donate K2 to the nation for all time by presenting it to the museum of the United Services Institution in 1843. This was a generous gift to history since 50 guineas would be equivalent to more than a year's salary to a working man. Herbert at a later date, also thoughtfully paid for an engraved inscription on the back of K2:

Presented to
THE UNITED SERVICES INSTITUTION
By
REAR ADMIRAL SIR THOMAS HERBERT, K.C.B., M.P.
This Timekeeper belonged to Captn. Cook, R.N.,
and was taken by him to Pacific in 1776
It was again taken to the Pacific by Captain
Bligh in the "Bounty" 1787
It was taken by the Mutineers to Pitcairn's Island
and was sold in 1808 by Adams to a citizen of
the United States,
who sold it at Chilli, where
it was purchased by
Sir Thomas Herbert.[174]

The inscription is a thrilling story. Herbert did well, although with the benefit of time, we can identify errors in the inscription.

---

[174] The inscription was engraved after 1852 when Herbert had been promoted

The marine chronometer used by Captain Cook was Kendall's K1 which was a direct copy of John Harrison's H4 which had been a condition of the Board of Longitude.

Cook never even saw K2 which was deliberately made to a lower but cheaper specification. The horologist Peter Amis, pointed out in 1957 that Kendall had made the "cardinal error of dispensing with the train remontoire" to save money. Larcum Kendall must have been technically aware of this, but took a commercial decision.

The second error was that K2 was clearly not sold to Captain Folger. It was handed over by Adams at the last moment as a gift. The well-bred Folger simply pulled out a silk handkerchief and added a few ship's items as gifts in return.

The third error on the inscription is that the "citizen of the United States" certainly did not sell K2 to the Spanish in 'Chilli'. Whereas Mayhew Folger would have called it piracy, the local Spanish militia believed they had a right to confiscate it.

While at the USI, K2 would sometimes be lent to other organisations and exhibitions. In 1876, the South Kensington Museum held a major exhibition of scientific instruments and equipment. The descriptive paragraph of K2 in the exhibition is fascinating:

"1840, was bought by Sir Thomas Herbert for 50 guineas. It was repaired and rated at Valparaiso and taken by Sir Thomas to China, and brought home in the *Blenheim* in 1843 'having kept a fair rate with the other chronometers for the space of three years'."[175]

On K2's 9th and last voyage, it was kept for nearly three years on two warships and compared with a number of modern maritime chronometers in war – and performed well.

Although K2 was on display from 1844, the actual inscription must have been engraved in England after 1852 when Herbert became an MP for Dartmouth and a Rear Admiral. It remained on display in the Royal United Services Institution until 1963, when the RUSI museum closed and the watch was transferred to the National Maritime Museum in Greenwich.

---

[175] Cambridge University Press, digitized

Royal Observatory Greenwich

The Royal Observatory Greenwich (ROG) in London is on the top of a hill in the Royal Park overlooking the National Maritime Museum (NMM). The Observatory has breathtaking views across large parts of London and the NMM is also stunningly located on lower flatter ground adjoining other world famous architectures and the historic River Thames. Both are now part of Royal Museums Greenwich.

John Harrison's famous pioneering marine timekeepers; H1, H2, H3 and H4 are all in good working order and on display in the Longitude gallery in the ROG, unless being lent for exhibitions. Harrison's final marine timekeeper H5 rests in a proud position in the collection of the Worshipful Company of Clockmakers.

Kendall's successful K1 which was referred to by Captain Cook as "our trusty friend the watch" was returned to Greenwich in 1802. The lower specification timekeeper K3 which had a target cost of £100 did have active and exciting service in Australia and the Arctic and much later also came back to

Greenwich. Eventually, K2 'The Bounty Watch' completed its final journey and took its place on display in 1963, as part of the collection.

Since Herbert decided to return to Britain via The Cape of Good Hope instead of Cape Horn, K2 never did circumnavigate the world – by just a few degrees. Bligh didn't get far enough west trying to round the Horn; Herbert was moored in Santiago; and the only evidence of the mule's furthest travels to the east is Santiago.

The International Prime Meridian at Greenwich, Zero degrees Longitude, runs through the Royal Observatory where the Harrisons are kept and displayed to visitors from all parts of the world. There is daily excitement and chatter in countless languages, as visitors make their way to the cobbled courtyard where the Greenwich Meridian line is marked so they can line up and put one foot on either side. One in the west. One in the east.

After Larcum Kendall had completed his three large marine watches, he focussed his high quality workmanship on assisting John Arnold with his designs and efforts to produce a new generation of affordable chronometers. He never produced any further K versions but the three Kendall marine timekeepers he built were vital stepping stones in navigation and the 'story of time'.

Retired mariner Peter Poland summarised: "Their performance was remarkable and set a standard for subsequent makers to aim for." Also, "Their success proved that the method of determining longitude at sea by chronometers was both practical and achievable"[176].

Kendall died on the 22 November 1790 aged 71 and being born into a Quaker family, was subsequently buried in the Kingston, Surrey Quaker cemetery.[177] His workshop, tools, parts and instruments were auctioned off on 23 December 1790, the proceeds going to his brother Moses and extended family.

K2 was lucky to survive the first 4 voyages. The journeys started with an Arctic expedition which was probably just hours away from destruction. The 2nd and 3rd voyages were in active

---

[176] Peter Poland, 1991 Travels of a Timekeeper, p18
[177] NNM Collections, Richard Dunn

190

war zones in North America where the ships and personnel were continually attacked by a resourceful enemy with fire and powder boats, floating bombs, cannons, submarine and violent plots. The 4th voyage was off the coast of equatorial West Africa where the Commander died of fever and K2 was transferred to a small frigate moving in uncharted shallow waters seeking a sanctuary for freed slaves.

Although Kendall would have known about the *Bounty* sailing in 1787 with his K2, he would never have known about the mutineers fighting to keep K2, its stay at Pitcairn and the overall violent outcome of the *Bounty* voyage.

Kendall might well have been intrigued that the Bounty Watch, so carefully built with his own Quaker hands, was subsequently rescued from Pitcairn by American Captain Mayhew Folger's Quaker hands in 1808. K2 was then forcibly pirated away by the Spanish, hauled along the Andes on a mule but decades later returned to the British in 1840 in South America by a friend of Charles Darwin. It was then shipped back from the New World via fierce China wars, before finally settling at the Royal Observatory, Greenwich, in 1963 and subsequently moved to the National Maritime Museum in 2018.

Who would have thought that after transferring K2 from Greenwich to Bligh's *Bounty* in 1787, it would take over 175 years before it actually returned to Greenwich – 'the home of time'.

Where it belongs!

Captain Folger on Pitcairn

200th Anniversary of the
Discovery of a Community

In 1808 Captain Mayhew Folger of the US Topaz came across the Pitcairn Island community while resting in the South East Pacific. He was the first contact the dwindling population had with civilisation since their arrival on the *Bounty*. John Adams was the sole survivor of the mutineers and he welcomed Folger, giving him Bligh's famous Kendall K2 chronometer.

Although Folger reported the discovery in late 1808, it was contained relatively unimportant by the British Admiralty, through until 1814 when Pitcairn was 'rediscovered', ending 25 years of isolation.

192

Pitcairn Porcelain given to Captain Folger with K2

Map First Opium War Conflict Overview 1839-42

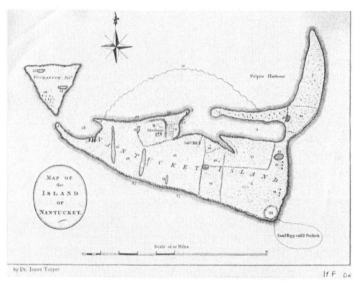

Map of the Island of Nantucket

Destroying Chinese War Junks 30th May 1843

Epilogue
Fletcher Christian
The Conspiracy Theory

Couldn't be done! Mission Impossible! Old Wives Tale! These are typical and understandable comments about the theory that Christian escaped from Pitcairn's Island and returned home to Britain. Fletcher 'died' countless times on Pitcairn's Island and there is still no body or grave. It had all the ingredients of a good Agatha Christie mystery.

One must consider that when Pitcairn was rediscovered, there was only one mutineer left. He was the crafty old sailor who called himself Alex Smith when his real name was John or Jack Adams. He may well have had good reason to hide his real name when signing up for the *Bounty* voyage, but it's also indicative of how his mind worked.

Captain Folger was first to rediscover Pitcairn's Island and his initial comments are significant, since they were the freshest memories of 'Alex Smith' (Aleck in Pitcairn). Folger's log book was limited but included: "from 1790...after which one of their party went mad and drowned himself another died with a fever and after they remained about 4 years on the Island, their servants rose up and killed six of them, leaving only Smith alive."[178]

Folger asked to see Fletcher Christian's grave, but the request was refused.

Folger later provided more detail in a meeting with Quaker merchant friends Samuel Coates and his wife in Philadelphia, who took notes of the conversation. The date would have been between 1811 and 1813.[179]

---

[178] Topaz Log Book
[179] Coates undated Letter

"In one or two years after the Company arrived in the Island one of them died of sickness and one jumped off the rocks in a fit of insanity, leaving only 7 of the mutineers."

The rest of the letter confirmed Folger's earlier version of the Otaheite servant's uprising. Neither version mentioned mutineer Edward Young, who apparently also survived the massacre.

In Folger's letter to the Admiralty when returning the azimuth compass, he included a paragraph: *"About six years after at this place, their servants attacked and killed all the English except the informant, and he was severely wounded."* The inference was that Christian was among the English killed in the uprising, which is still the conventional wisdom of how he died.[180]

While the ship *Topaz* was close to Pitcairn, there were communications between the *Topaz* crew and the young Pitcairners, who helped to load barrels of water on the ship. The *Topaz* second mate later reported to Lieutenant Fitzmaurice in Chile that he was informed by the young men "that Christian, the ring leader became insane shortly after their arrival on the island and threw himself off the rocks into the sea. Another mutineer died of fever before the massacre"[181].

Christian's name was now connected to the 'suicide on the rocks and sea' version of death. Such information behind the scenes by young Pitcairners could well be more accurate than the formal one given to strangers from a complex and anxious old man.

The explorer Delano later met up in Boston with Folger, who was very specific that "Christian became sick and died a natural death, and it was after this when the Otaheitan men joined in a conspiracy…"[182]. This seems to place Christian as being the one with fever, instead of jumping into the sea – but still before the Polynesian's massacre.

The next ship to arrive at Pitcairn in October 1814 was the *Briton* under Sir Thomas Staines and Captain Pipon. They spent

---

[180] Folger's Admiralty letter about compass
[181] Delano, Ch.5
[182] Ibid

much more time than Folger on the Island and Staines wrote a letter to Vice Admiral Dixon about his visit. The version of Christian's death from Alex Smith to Staines was: "His Otaheitan wife died within a twelve month from their landing, after which he carried off one (wife) that belonged to an Otaheitan man, who watched for an opportunity of taking his revenge and shot him dead while digging his own field."[183]

This version indicates that the killing of Christian was an individual personal vendetta, which took place before or during the main uprising.

Some months after landing, John William's wife fell off the cliffs to her death while looking for bird's eggs. After some time, Williams grew restless and demanded one of the three women allocated to the six Polynesian men. Initially, the other mutineers refused but Williams threatened "to leave Pitcairn in the ship's cutter"[184]. Christian was deemed to lead an armed party to take away one of the Island women for Williams. Trouble was inevitable, but Christian might well have done this for a *Bounty* sailor, if not for himself.

The threat by Williams to escape on the *Bounty* cutter may well have planted seeds in Fletcher's mind. An experienced sailor like Christian should have been able to cope with the cutter. Christian had plenty of time in his hide-away to brood and plot.

Following the uprising and subsequent killings, Smith and Edward Young were the only two Europeans left. They presumably became very close and Young is reputed to have taught Smith how to read and write. Young would have taken over Christian's role of looking after the navigational equipment including K2.

For over a year they were inseparable and both were aware of Young's declining health. It was up to them to decide what Island history to tell the world, since none of the women spoke English. They would want history to see them and the mutineers in a good light and must have agreed on a joint story. Young's documents appeared much later and he took the line that

---

[183] Staines letter to Admiralty and Delano, Ch.5
[184] Gavin Kennedy, About Bligh, p105

Christian died in the uprising. This must have been discussed with Smith, who subsequently wavered.

One of the Polynesian women called Jenny had been married to Isaac Martin, the only American in the *Bounty* mutiny. She left Pitcairn in April 1810 on the American ship *Sultan* to Chile under Captain Rogers and sometime later, she returned to Tahiti. She dictated her story to Captain Rogers who spoke Polynesian and also to Mr Nott, a missionary.

Jenny's story included Christian's death happening in the main uprising. This is, indeed, credible, but there is still no supporting evidence or physical proof. Did she even have her own motives? Did she really want the world to know that their leader and kidnapper, successfully escaped from the Island?

After the uprising, bodies were lying around or buried where they fell or carried to a communal pit, but there still appears to be little proof of who is where. Of all the deaths that Christian was supposed to have suffered, one of them was essentially very different to the others. Killing himself from the cliffs is the only death that wouldn't necessarily leave a body. Everyone could believe that it had been swept away by the sea.

The Conspiracy Theory includes the idea of John Williams, who threatened to leave the Island in the *Bounty* cutter unless he had a wife. After Christian's wife Isabella died, he had plenty of time to plan, build up provisions and ensure the cutter or even a larger canoe was in reasonable condition and easily accessible before sailing out at night.

Christian was a strong and experienced sailor and all he needed was to meet up with or hail a passing merchant ship, whaler or sealer. He could pay gold ducats or work his passage. He could sell or donate the cutter to facilitate travelling to other lands, before discretely returning to England and his family.

What trail in Pitcairn could he leave? The obvious one was leaving a few clothes at the top of a cliff as evidence he was mad and killed himself. That is a well-known practice today which includes a British Member of Parliament, insurance fraudsters and a variety of individuals who wanted to disappear.

Why didn't he take K2 with him? That would have been too obvious and he had sufficient navigation kit. Even if the remaining Europeans on the Island suspected something, declaring that Christian the leader had deserted, it would have been a devastating blow to the Island's morale.

Fiona Mountain on her web page noted: "The *Bounty's* cutter strangely disappears from the Pitcairn chronicles."[185] Furthermore, there is much general comment that William Wordsworth helped Christian's lawyer brother Edward, to prepare the defence of Christian in his absence. It has been commented that Coleridge, another family friend who wrote the 'The Rime of the Ancient Mariner', also wrote to the press using information that only Christian would know.

All these friends and family had a motive to protect Fletcher but there is no proof of giving him sanctuary. However, author Glynn Christian discovered that after Professor Edward Christian died in 1823, he surprisingly left no will. This absence of a will was repeated by other members of the Christian family, despite their family's legal connections. There is a question whether Fletcher Christian had "lived on, the secret recipient of his dead family's possessions"[186].

Something which has real substance is that Captain Peter Heywood believed and was adamant, that he saw Christian in Plymouth. Peter was a midshipman on the *Bounty* who was a close friend of Fletcher and had stayed with the mutineers when returning to Tahiti. He remained on Tahiti and was subsequently rounded up and judged in England. Although found guilty, he was pardoned by the king, probably because of his age and powerful friends.

In some ways, Christian would have been reasonably safe in public since there were no photographs being shown on television or in newspapers. Only a sailing mate or family would really recognise him.

In 1831, Sir John Barrow interviewed Peter Heywood who was by then a captain in the Royal Navy and he published in detail the interview, referring to a sighting in about 1809:

"In Fore Street, Plymouth Dock, Captain Heywood found himself one day walking behind a man, whose shape had so much appearance of Christian's that he involuntarily quickened

---

[185] Fiona Mountain web
[186] Glyn Christian, Fragile Paradise, p194

his pace. Both were walking very fast and the rapid steps behind him having roused the stranger's attention, he suddenly turned his face, looked at Heywood and immediately ran off. But the face was as much like Christian's as the back, and Heywood, exceedingly excited, ran also. Both ran as fast as they were able; but the stranger had the advantage, and after making several short turns, disappeared."[187]

It would be natural to run, if the alternative was a possible public hanging. As a good friend, Heywood waited many years before releasing this information. No one has suggested that Captain Heywood was lying but critics over 100 years later say that "he was mistaken" or "age diminished his memory". How could they know? Most people can recognise close contacts by their movement, stature, walking and general demeanour without seeing a face. Heywood would have known every pimple on Christian. He saw his body shape and was also face to face with only a few inches between them.

There was no way that Christian could take the risk of recognition to a uniformed naval officer, who had a legal duty to hand him in for trial. The fact the officer was chasing him, would only have increased Christian's fear.

---

[187] Sir John Barrow, 1831

Captain Heywood 1822.

There are reports that Adams claimed that he accidentally shot Christian while he was trying to escape in a boat. This is very interesting and puts Christian back in the boat / suicide location near the rocks of the sea. One would think that Fletcher would flee at night, but this story admits that an escape by sea was a credible option.[188]

This claim appears to include a 'convenient' promise from the dying Christian that Adams should bury him in a secret grave on the Island. It would surely have been difficult to kill someone, drag the body around, dig a hole and then fill it with earth, without anyone noticing. Indeed, the community might wonder where he was.

---

[188] Gavin Kennedy, p117, and Glyn Christian, p195

Show us the money! The leading currency in the South Pacific at these times were Dutch gold ducats which were supplied to the *Bounty* and kept safely in the large cabin under Bligh's control. Bligh's orders on 20 November 1787, when referring to buying local goods, included "with the ducats with which you have also been furnished for that purpose". It appears that this money has never been accounted for.[189]

Since Bligh had been taken in the *Bounty* mutiny in only his night gown, it would have been challenging for him to hide the gold ducats. After the mutiny, Christian occupied the large cabin, so the money would have been under his control. Where is the money now? There can only be two credible possibilities. Either it was taken by Christian to pay for a new life or it is still on Pitcairn's Island.

Christian would never have left without the money. While on the Island he would have hidden it well. It wouldn't be where farmers could dig it up or stumble upon. A safer place for example, would be on a cliff face. He could have lowered himself on a rope to stash and recover the ducats when needed. Indeed, it was William's wife who fell off the cliffs. Was she really looking for golden eggs?

Fletcher Christian's death is still a mystery. Nothing has been satisfactorily proven either way. If the valuable stash of gold ducats is ever found on Pitcairn's Island, it would prove that Christian died on the Island. If not, without any DNA evidence or new manuscripts, it is clearly arguable that the Conspiracy Theory does have real substance.

---

[189] Fiona Mountain web

The Killing Fields

This book illustrates that Captain Mayhew Folger of Nantucket would never have found Pitcairn's Island and K2, unless he was a sealer. This global business was vital to ports such as Nantucket. There was an inevitable hunting side, which was brutal and bloody. Folger's target preys were fur seals and sea elephants. He had to find them, kill them and skin them. Unless this subject is of specific interest, please avoid this chapter.

Hunting Target One: Fur Seals

Seals are marine mammalian creatures classed as 'Pinnipedia' or 'fin-footed'. They are subdivided into 'eared' and 'earless' seals and the fur seal firmly belong to the 'eared' category. The fur seal is probably the most attractive of seals with a small head, small ears and bewitching eyes. The large rotund liquid pools of eyes evolved to seize any glint of light in ocean depths. The lips are not flabby and overhanging but firmly lined – like humans. They eat fish, krill and squid.

Their upper lip supports a white /grey moustache with long stiff bristles which can sweep over their shoulders like a plume. The bristles are there to help them hunt fish and squid in the dark. Long seal whiskers were valued in China for cleaning opium pipes. Fur seals are intelligent, playful and hold their head high out of the water. Their fore feet or flippers are dark bluish – black which they can lift up and gallop in short bursts, dragging their hind feet behind them.

Sea Otters had the most luxurious fur for the Canton market but quality fur seal pelts were also valued. Fur seals have two coats. One is a short crisp glistening overfur or guard hair which the animals continuously groom, while the inner one is a soft elastic pelage that gives value to the pelt. New techniques developed in London around 1800 to remove the outer guard, significantly increased the demand for these furs.

Male or Bull: A prime male of 3–4 years is about 6–7 feet from the tip of his nose to the bottom of his abbreviated tail. He would weigh about 400 lbs although older ones could grow to 500–600 lbs. Early in the season he would have a heavy neck of blubber which he would live off during the ensuing battles.

Although the actual breeding season is mainly October to January, the southern males can arrive as early as April, well before the females, to establish their territory for harems. This probably averages about 10 cows but particularly large and fierce males such as the 'beach masters' can have harems of 50 or more, leaving numerous smaller, lonely bachelor male seals occupying the sides of the colonies.

Female or Cow: The females are significantly smaller, at about 4 feet in length, weighing about 70–100 lbs. They bear a single pup very soon after arriving at the grounds and are ready to mate soon after the pup's birth.

Sailors on long journeys with 'male-only' company have long fantasised about erotic sea images. There were the ancient Greek Sirens with angelic songs luring men to a watery grave. Sailors have mistaken dugongs as mermaids languishing on rocks.

The female fur seal has been acclaimed as a beautiful creature with 'an expressive pair of large hazel blue eyes' and a female sleekness around the neck as she is poised in an upright posture. The countenance of the face and small head is gentle and reflective of her mood.[190] She shows maternal instincts in pitifully trying to protect her pups behind her flippers, when being surrounded by violent men.

---

[190] Henry W Elliott, The Seal Islands of Alaska, U.S. Department of Interior, 1881

THE COUNTENANCE OF CALLORHINUS.—A LIFE STUDY OF AN ADULT MALE FUR-SEAL.
(Full face of old male, profile and under view of female heads.)
Drawing by Henry W. Elliott, North Rookery, Pribylov Group, July 5, 1872. op. 73.)

Countenance of Female Fur Seal.

Tools of the Trade: The basic killing tools for fur seals were:

- Strong hard wood clubs of oak or hickory about 5–6 feet long.
- Stabbing knives.
- Flensing knives.
- Sharpening stones or butcher steels.

There were also optional 'Hakapik' clubs which are a cross between a club and an ice pick. It is a lethal Norwegian tool with a wedge iron head on one side to crush a seal's skull and a sharp hooked spike on the other side to drag the carcase along. This would be handy in icy conditions. If a seal is spiked through the neck or head, it protects the pelt.

Hakapik Club

The Onslaught: The first to be killed were usually the cows because of the superior fur. The typical approach was for small groups of the sealing team to surround a convenient number of female seals, possibly still with their guarding bull. The teams would start hitting the seals with their hard wood clubs on the skulls to knock them unconscious or kill them. The males were usually last to be stunned since they could be useful in keeping their harem together.

If only stunned, seals would then be killed by the stabbing knife being plunged into their chests to the heart. The batch of seals would then be lined up and pups hiding under their mother's flippers could be dragged out and dispatched.

The Flensing knives would then be drawn to cut the seals pelt so that the skin can be torn off in one piece from the carcase. This could compare in speed with sheep shearing.

The Flensing knife would generally continue to be used for 'beaming' or scraping the skin clean of any blood and flesh remaining on the skin – usually when the pelt was stretched or pegged out. The sealers would then move on to another convenient group of seals. Although some seals would make 'a dash for it', they would lie exhausted and trembling after just 30 yards. This may be a result of fur seals not having sweat glands.

Before the fresh pelts are ready for packing they would need to be air dried or salted or both. Salting could be carried out later on the vessel or on shore. In the case of large-scale harvesting, a whole team could be left on shore for some months.

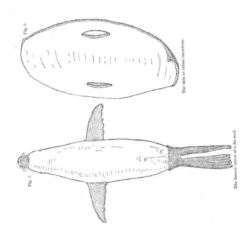

The Fleeced Carcase of a Fur Seal and the Separated Pelt.

Bachelor Seals: Although the skins of many bull beachmaster seals would be flawed from numerous fights over females, full grown bachelor seals tended to be in prime condition and, being larger than the females, were highly valuable commercial targets.

In some locations, northern fur seals in particular could be driven in large groups of a couple of hundreds, to a more convenient and spacious killing field, before being methodically slaughtered and skinned.

Fur Seal Physiology: Why was it all too easy for the sealers? It was the bones. The soft bones! The fur seal's skull is small and soft and can be easily crushed with one stroke of the hickory and oak clubs.

Danger to Crews: It was not all one way. There was danger to the sealing crews involved in heavy bloody work, in slippery conditions, using sharp weapons in a noisy environment. There would be non-stop raucous screaming from the seals. Although the clubbed seals were supposed to be unconscious or dead, they regularly managed to bite their executioners on the ankles and hands which sometimes led to missing fingers, 'Sealer's Fingers'.

With regards to man, the bull fur seals were always on the defensive. They wouldn't openly attack but nor would they easily retreat.

Crews sometimes complained about receiving sharp stings while clubbing the seals. Further research in Alaska by Henry W Elliot concluded it was the eyes. The seal's eyes. "The seal's heads are stricken so hard sometimes that those crystalline lenses to their eyes fly out from the orbital sockets like hail stones, or little pebbles, and frequently struck me sharply in the face or elsewhere, while I stood nearby watching the killing gang at work."[191]

Different breeds of seal reacted quite differently. Sea Horses (Walruses) were known for getting upset when stabbed and could try to splinter a wooden boat.

George Vancouver's expedition to survey NW America in 1792 suffered unforgiving revenge from a den of sea lions in the Falklands. Captain New "met up with a sea lion who he affronted by firing a charge of small Shot at him. The lion, instead of retreating, followed so closely that I was glad to repair to the Boat but the lion followed the Boat all the way to the Ship. Following further shots at this lion, the Captain confessed he was "more fright than he ever was before"[192].

In the case of Nantucket and possibly all New England, most of the ship owners and officers were of Quaker stock, who freed their slaves 100 years before the rest of America. Yet these humane people must have wrestled in long, quiet meetings about their brutal business and the rights of animals and the scale of their exploitation of fellow mammals.

Crews doing the actual bloody work were a mixed bunch. They were the lowest echelon in mariner status. In addition to

[191] Henry W Elliott, The Seal Islands of Alaska, U.S. Department of Interior, 1881
[192] NMM Board of Longitude. CUDL ref: MS/MM/6/48

local whites and native Indians, many were recruited from the Azores, Madeira and Cape Verde.

When America drew up regulations in the mid-19th century protecting the rights of sailors, they specifically excluded sealing crews.

Fur Seal Oil: This was not of high quality or, indeed, quantity from the fast swimming fur seals and so the oil would often be ignored when on fur hunts. If taken, the blubber would be boiled in three-legged metal try pots, either on-board or on-shore. The carcases were generally left to rot.

Hunting Target Two: The Sea Elephant

The term 'Sea Elephant' was generally used in the 18th century but changed to 'Elephant Seal' once the hunting turned into a global oil business.

Northern Elephant Seal

The elephant seal is the largest of the pinnipeds. This gentle creature had been largely ignored in the early seal-rush, but with an increased demand for quality oils coinciding with a decline of the overhunted sperm whale, elephant seals became a prime target. The oil from the elephant seal was second only to the mighty sperm whale for quality and price.

The bull elephant seals were considerably bigger and heavier than the cow. The former would typically weigh about 8000 pounds to the lighter 2000 pounds of the cow. Generally, the bigger they are, the deeper they dive.[193]

Tools of the Trade: Although the same clubs used on fur seals were handy, the basic killing tools were different with the elephant seal.

- Long metal-tipped lances.
- Muskets.
- Long flensing knives.
- Some clubs – for killing young pups.

Muskets were rarely used on fur seals because of potential damage to the fur pelt. The exception was pelagic hunting of seals when as many dead seals sank at sea having been shot, as were hauled out the water.

Muskets were, however, extensively used on elephant seals. From 1750 to 1850 – these would have generally been smooth bore, muzzle loaded guns with a flint lock firing mechanism. In cold weather, the ram rods for compressing the gun powder between shots could be slow. After the end of the American Civil War, new rifles became available with breach loaded metal cartridges and a rifled barrel with superior muzzle velocity. These would be much more efficient and accurate tools to ensure a quick clean kill to the head.

The long barrelled Kentucky rifle was based on a unique German design and particularly popular with 'sharp shooters'. Although a flintlock muzzle-loader, it had a rifled barrel long before breach loading guns were available. It spun the lead bullet for accuracy and projectile stability, but was slower to reload than a smooth bore.

The hide of the elephant seal had limited financial value. In the late 18th and early 19th centuries, the blubber processing was wasteful. The flensed carcasses were often abandoned on the fields, although the hides were sometimes used for belts, wallets, harnesses and various covers.

---

[193] April 1987, National Geographic, Roger L Gentry

Tactics: The simplest hunting tactic was to shoot them in the head. If the animal was upright and moving, long lances would facilitate a killing stroke to the throat. If the herd was asleep, the killing noises seemed not to awaken the herd, so the sealers could methodically kill one after the other at leisure.

If the herd was fully awake, there would be much bellowing and short bursts of movement while the bull seals would try to keep their harem together. One tactic was to blind the bull seals in one eye so they could only focus on controlling their harem.

These creatures were particularly vulnerable because of their tameness and habit in congesting in large groups and like all seals, they have to come out of the water to breed. Another survival weakness of seals is that they generally hunt at night and sleep by day.

The thick hide would typically have about one foot of blubber, depending on the season. This would be removed in convenient strips about two foot square called 'horse-pieces'. Such chunks would be minced before boiling in metal try pots on the beach or boat. Flensing methods could be used and sometimes heavy weights were placed on the blubber to force it through a strainer.[194]

Anything available was used to fuel the fires including penguin skins and bits of seal skin and blubber scraps left over.

Because of the weight of each animal, the sealers would sometimes attempt to move them to one end of the beach where they could be trapped near the try pots. They could then be butchered before cutting up the 12" thick blubber for boiling into commercial oil. The rest of the carcase including skin, meat, bones and offal was generally left behind.

Oil casks would generally be brought in as 'flat packs' and assembled into complete barrels on arrival. Oil extraction techniques improved over time until the average Elephant seal produced enough oil for 2 barrels totalling about 80 imperial gallons.

Season: In the case of southern elephant seals, the males would often arrive in August to claim and hold their territory.

---

[194] AB Dickinson, Seal Fisheries of the Falklands, Research in Maritime History No. 34

213

The pregnant cows would follow in September and October with the pups being born about a week after coming ashore. They would be part of a harem and after 18 days after giving birth, they would start an optimum fertility time lasting 4 days, when mating took place.[195]

Most breeding animals would leave at the end of November although moulting specimens, juveniles and loners could still appear through the winter.

The most productive time for taking oil from bulls is about September, before the bull loses weight through the fasting period. Excluding blood, some 20–25% of a mature bull is blubber, of which about 60–70% is pure oil, which could command high prices.

Blood: Much of the killing would be on open beaches before winter had sent in. Some of this work was in snowy conditions. There was comment on the 'brightness' of the seal blood against the white snow. Recent studies indicate that because seals need to dive hundreds and even thousands of feet deep in the oceans for their food, they need much more haemoglobin in their blood.

This was sealer's business. It's what they did and what nations are still doing. However, one of them rediscovered Pitcairn's Island, solved the mystery of the missing *Bounty* mutineers and "launched K2 on yet another round of adventures"[196].

[195] Richard M Laws, Biology of Antarctic Seals
[196] Dava Sobel, Longitude, p154

Appendix
Kendall and Harrison's Technology
By Mike Dryland

Larcum Kendall made three watches for the Board of Longitude in response to John Harrison's work. Kendall's first watch, 'K1', is an almost exact copy of H4, Harrison's famous 4th marine timekeeper.

Harrison's story has already been told comprehensively by Rupert Gould, Humphrey Quill, Dava Sobel, Jonathan Betts and others. It is not our intention to replicate it here. This summary is offered as a background to the account of K2's travels. Readers wanting more detail should consult the excellent works listed in the Bibliography.

Harrison's achievement was all the more remarkable for his background. He had only a primary education and no university degree. He was a carpenter (cabinet maker really) born in Yorkshire in 1693 and raised in Lincolnshire. Everything he knew about science and technology he taught himself from books and his own experiments. Harrison also taught himself clock making – he served no apprenticeship. Just as well, or he would have known that what he set himself to do was thought impossible.

By the time he was about 30 years old, Harrison was making some of the best pendulum clocks in the world, accurate to a second a month. Their 'movements' (the clockwork), he made mainly from wood using his carpentry skills. Harrison's domestic clocks are remarkable for three innovations –

- First, he went to great lengths to eliminate friction from the mechanism as much as possible. He avoided sliding friction (rubbing parts) and made all moving parts to be rolling on curved surfaces. In particular, he devised a new escapement mechanism, the 'grasshopper' which operates free of sliding friction. (A clock's *escapement* is the mechanism which keeps the clock ticking in time and also keeps the pendulum going by giving it a little push on each swing – Harrison's 'grasshopper' is so-called because its action resembles the back legs of the insect).

- Second, he built clocks which didn't require oil. In Harrison's day, there was no good oil such as we take for granted. Only animal fats like goose grease were available and these soon became sticky and made the clock slow down and require quite frequent cleaning. Eliminating friction removed the need for much oil and Harrison also used a tropical hardwood, lignum vitae, which is naturally oily, to make the bushes (bearings) and rollers.

- Third, he invented a new and effective way to cancel out temperature change. When a pendulum clock heats up, the pendulum will expand (lengthen) and swing more slowly (the time of swing of a pendulum depends on its length) and the clock will itself slow down and lose time. Harrison knew that brass expands more than steel, and he devised a pendulum of alternating brass and steel rods arranged so that they expanded (or contracted) in opposite directions to each other and kept the length of the pendulum unchanged as temperature altered. This 'gridiron' pendulum was a world-first. To design the gridiron Harrison had performed his own experiments to measure carefully the coefficients of expansion of brass and steel.

When he arrived in London, he hadn't yet actually made a sea clock, but his ideas won over the Astronomer Royal, Edmond Halley, and also London's leading clock- and instrument-maker, George Graham. They became Harrison's friends and mentors and helped him through his early trials and tribulations and dealings with the Board of Longitude. After Halley and Graham died, his relationship with the Board was never so cordial.

Living almost exclusively on loans from the Board (to be repaid later) Harrison built a series of four machines now preserved for all to see at the Royal Observatory Greenwich.

The first three, now known as H1, H2 and H3, are large machines of brass and steel. Each stands roughly 2 feet tall (c 60 cm) and they weigh between 66 lbs (H3) and 103 lbs (H2) – 30 to 47 kg.

Harrison's starting points were his large land clocks, accurate to a second a month, achieved with the radical innovations described above, but he had to solve additional major problems to be able to keep accurate time aboard a ship at sea –

- A pendulum won't work on a pitching, rolling ship at sea and couldn't be used. To cancel the movement of the ship on H1 and H2, he used 'twin bar balances' (like brass dumbbells) cross-connected, rocking in opposite directions to each other and controlled by steel springs. Any movement of the ship that disturbs one balance will act in the opposite direction on the other and be cancelled out.

- Harrison had to devise a way to use his gridiron temperature compensation in the sea clocks. They do not have a pendulum but as the clock heats up the steel springs controlling the twin balances of H1 and H2 will expand and loosen and the clock will slow down. It is believed he attempted to integrate a gridiron into the bar balances themselves but failed to do so to his satisfaction. Instead he fitted the gridirons so that they acted through levers onto the steel springs controlling the balances – they automatically tightened or loosened the springs (so to speak), speeding-up or slowing-down the clock to cancel temperature change.

- For H3 the gridiron was refined into the 'bimetallic strip', a world-first invention still used today in electric kettles and toasters – most thermostats.

- H1, 2 and 3 contain all Harrison's ingenious devices to eliminate friction and the clocks require no oil – a particular advantage for sea clocks which need to run accurately, without stopping (or cleaning), for the length of the voyage. Among his innovations in H3 was a low-friction bearing, the 'caged roller race', which is the ancestor of today's ball bearing race.

Harrison borrowed money from George Graham, returned home to Lincolnshire and took about six years to build and adjust H1. After himself trying H1 at sea with promising results in 1736, the Board loaned him another £250 to make a second improved sea clock. Harrison moved his family to London and took just under three years to build H2. During this time he realised the action of the twin bar balances in H1 and H2 was flawed – certain movements of the ship would slow the clock. The Board was persuaded to loan more money and in 1741 he embarked on H3, his 'curious 3rd machine'. To correct the flaw the bar balances were replaced by large twin balance wheels (circular balances) cross-connected and swinging in opposite directions to each other.

In total, Harrison toiled almost twenty years on H3 but failed to make it run to his satisfaction. After fourteen years, he decided he was on the wrong track – such large machines, beating seconds, were too vulnerable to the rolling and pitching of a ship at sea.

He resolved to make some watches – small, portable timekeepers. He realised that a watch, relatively small compared to H1, 2 and 3, and with a relatively massive, fast-beating balance, would be less affected by the motion of the ship. He had reversed his entire approach – from first trying to make a large accurate clock be portable, he now set out to make a small portable watch be accurate at sea.

To begin, wanting an accurate pocket watch for himself, he had designed a watch containing many of his innovations. It was built for him by an associate, John Jefferys. Known as the 'Jefferys Watch', it now resides in the collection of the Worshipful Company of Clockmakers in London. Completed around 1753, the excellent performance of the Jefferys Watch gave Harrison the confidence to request another loan from the Board to continue his work on watches.

In 1759, about 30 years after starting work on H1, the result was his 4th marine timekeeper, H4, a large watch 5 inches (125 mm) in diameter, weighing about 3 lbs (1.4 kg), housed in a splendid solid silver pair-case (i.e. a double case). It featured Harrison's bimetallic temperature compensation, a single balance wheel and jewelled bearings.

Harrison knew that in principle the temperature compensation should be fitted to the moving parts of the balance itself, but he failed to achieve this. Instead the bimetallic strip in H4 is fitted outside the balance. It was left to Harrison's successors to invent a proper compensated balance.

Like the Jefferys Watch, H4's balance beats five times a second – five times faster than H1, 2 and 3. Harrison's fast-beating balance was his primary innovation contributing to accurate timekeeping at sea. He realised that a fast beating balance would have much more energy (momentum) and be far less affected by the rolling and pitching of the ship.

Harrison flew in the face of convention with his design – at the time watchmakers believed a watch must be 'self-starting': as soon as you began to wind it up, it should start to run. To achieve this, a lighter balance wheel was the custom. Harrison had come to the conclusion that a lightweight balance was a poor design, being vulnerable to movement. Instead he used a relatively heavy, fast-beating, balance which would control the watch properly. This design, however, was not self-starting – after winding; it required a little sideways twist of the watch to set it running.

Harrison was unable to miniaturise the lignum vitae wood bushes used on H1, 2 and 3, and instead, jewelled bearings made with rubies and diamond end-stones were needed. Harrison was by no means the first to use jewelled bearings but H4 was the most extensively jewelled watch in the world when completed.

H4, like all of his marine timekeepers, is powered by a mainspring which runs 30 hours and so needs to be wound every day. A mainspring delivers more power when fully wound than when nearly run down and this will affect the timekeeping of the watch. Part of the remedy was an already existing mechanism called a 'fusee' – a thin chain connecting the spring barrel to the train of gears, it is wrapped around a cone. When the mainspring is fully wound the chain sits around the narrow end of the cone exerting less pull (moment). As the spring runs down, the chain unwinds toward the wide end of the cone, exerting more pull and compensating for the drop in power from the spring.

When the mainspring is in the act of being wound, however, the fusee will not deliver power and the watch will stop. To counteract this Harrison designed a new form of a mechanism called 'maintaining power' which provides power to run the watch while it is wound.

Lastly, to smooth the delivery of power to the escapement (the mechanism that makes the watch tick evenly) Harrison designed a new form of a device called a 'remontoire'. Without a remontoire, power from the mainspring has to be transmitted from gear to gear through the train of gears and finally is delivered somewhat jerkily to the escapement affecting the running of the watch. With a remontoire, power is delivered directly and evenly to the escapement from a secondary spring which is itself rewound at intervals automatically from the mainspring. H2, 3 and 4 each has a remontoire. In H4, it rewinds automatically every 7½ seconds.

As we have seen, H4 was tested twice on voyages to the West Indies by William Harrison, John's son. On the first trial to Jamaica in 1761-2, H4 performed much better than required to win the Longitude reward of £20,000 (over £6 million in modern buying power). John claimed the money, but was refused – the Board of Longitude knew many copies of H4 would be needed, but John would not explain its design and the Board couldn't tell if copies would be possible. The Board told the Harrisons that the trial had not been fair – there had been a technicality: the Harrisons hadn't declared in advance the 'rate' (the predictable error, fast or slow) of H4.

The Board insisted on a second trial and in 1764 William took the watch back, this time to Barbados. H4 performed even better – the results showed it was performing three times better than required to claim the £20,000 reward. The Board offered half the amount – £10,000, then a huge sum, but John would not accept. He accused the Board of trying to cheat him and a feud developed between the Harrisons and the Board while John fought to claim the full reward. He was first required to disclose the design and construction of H4, after which he was paid the first £10,000. He was now a rich man but he wasn't about to give up there.

To be considered for the full £20,000 reward Harrison was required by the Board to make two copies of H4 to show copies would be possible. John was now over 70 years old and knew he didn't have the time remaining to him to complete the work. He argued bitterly but the Board would not relent. All he could do was buckle down and work. From 1767 to 1770 John and William worked to make a 5th marine timekeeper, now called H5. H5 is outwardly different in appearance from H4, but its mechanism is very similar. It is preserved in the collection of the Clockmakers Company.

John's bad-tempered exchanges with the Board now convinced him that he would obtain no further satisfaction from there, and he decided instead to appeal to the king, George III. The Harrisons wrote for help in January 1772. King George, who loved science and technology, took up their cause and participated himself in a trial of H5 at his observatory in Kew, west of London. He was impressed by H5 and the plight of the Harrisons – "By God Harrison, I will see you righted!"

With the king's help, John Harrison appealed directly to the British Parliament over the heads of the Board of Longitude. In June 1773, by Act of Parliament, Harrison received the rest of the money. He was 80 years old.

At Greenwich, the astronomers had at last completed the work needed to compile the astronomical tables to enable navigators to find Greenwich Time from anywhere in the world by observations of the Moon. In 1766, the 5th Astronomer Royal, Nevil Maskelyne, published the 1st edition of the *Nautical Almanac and Astronomical Ephemeris*. The Almanac provided the apparent position of the Moon against the background of stars predicted at Greenwich Time every three hours through the following year. It represented the cumulative efforts of 90 years' work at Greenwich and incorporated new lunar tables from Tobias Mayer in Gottingen University in Hanover using theories of astronomer-mathematicians in Switzerland and France. Using the Almanac, navigators could calculate the time difference between local and Greenwich Time and find longitude. A new instrument, the 'sextant', developed from the earlier 'octant', suitable for use on a ship at sea, had appeared in 1757. It gave navigators at sea the means to measure accurately the angles seen between the Moon, horizon and nearby stars or Sun. Navigators now had a choice of two methods to find longitude – by 'lunars', or by 'chronometer' (sometimes logged as by timepiece 'TP').

Following the disclosure of H4's design, Harrison was required to surrender the watch to the Board. While he worked on his own copy (H5), the Board also decided to commission another from a different maker to see if Harrison's work could be independently reproduced. Larcum Kendall was chosen (a great honour) and H4 placed in his hands in May 1767. Kendall had the advantage of having worked with Harrison on H4. He delivered the copy, today called K1, to the Board in January 1770.

K1 is an almost exact copy of H4 'part for part'. Externally there are two small differences – the shape of the bow and screw heads on the dial. Internally the engraving on the cock and top plate differs from H4 and is if anything more beautiful and elaborate than the original. William Harrison was pleased to concede that the workmanship in K1 was superior to his father's in H4. Kendall was paid a total of £500 for K1 – a large sum, call it £30,000 in modern values.

The Board asked Kendall if he would be willing to train other watchmakers to make copies of H4 but he demurred. He thought the design of H4 to be too complex and expensive to be the basis for lots of copies. After some discussion, the Board commissioned Kendall to make a simpler watch, omitting the parts of Harrison's expensive mechanism which he, Kendall, thought unnecessary. It was to be made for £200.

K2 was completed in 1772. To simplify, Kendall decided to leave out Harrison's complex remontoire mechanism (see above), but this was a mistake. The performance of K2 never matched its predecessor, K1.

Kendall was also asked to make a 3rd watch, K3, delivered in 1774 at a cost of £100. The movement of K3 is similar to K2 but has a modified design of escapement, and externally K3 appears very different – it has three small dials, one each for hours, minutes and seconds. Like K2, K3 failed to measure up to the original H4/K1.

All three of Kendall's watches for the Board, K1, 2 and 3, are now in the collection of the National Maritime Museum at Greenwich.

Short Bibliography

Alexander, Caroline: *The Bounty*, 2003.

Amis, Peter: *The Bounty Timekeeper*, The Horological Journal, 1957.

Betts, Jonathan: *Harrison*, 1993 and later editions.

Betts, Jonathan: *Marine Chronometers at Greenwich*, 2018.

Bligh, William & Christian, Edward: *The Bounty Mutiny*, introduction by R.D. Madison, 2001.

Bligh, William: *Narrative of the Mutiny on Board H.M. Ship Bounty...* 1790.

Bligh, William: *Notebook* 1789, John Bach (Ed), 1985.

Bligh, William; Brunton, Paul (Ed): *Awake, bold Bligh! William Bligh's Letters describing the mutiny on HMS Bounty*, 1989.

Busch, Briton Cooper: *The War against the Seals*, 1985.

Christian, Glynn: *Mrs. Christian, 'Bounty' Mutineer*, 2011.

Christopher, Emma: *A Merciless Place – The fate of Britain's convicts after the American Revolution*, 2010.

Delano, Amasa: *Narrative of Voyages and Travels in the Northern and Southern Hemispheres* Vol.1 Boston, 1817.

Dickinson, Anthony Bertram.: *Seal Fisheries of Falkland Islands and Dependencies*, 2007.

Dunn, Richard & Higgit, Rebekah: *Finding Longitude*, 2014.

Dunn, Richard: *Navigational Instruments*, 2016.

Edwards, Edward (Capt.) & Hamilton, George (Surgeon): *Voyage of HMS Pandora...*, 1790-1.

Edwards, Phillip: *Journals of Captain Cook*, 1999.

Elliott, Henry Wood: *The Seal-islands of Alaska*, 1881.

Frank, Katherine: *Crusoe – Daniel Defoe, Robert Knox and the Creation of a Myth*, 2011.

Gould, Rupert T: *The Marine Chronometer – its History & Development*, London 1923 (new edition: Antique Collectors' Club 2013).

Grant, James: *British Battles on Land and Sea*, 1897.

Green, John Richard: *Short History of the English People*, Vol. IV 1894.

Hammerton, Sir John Alexander (Ed): *The Outline History of the World*, 1933.

Hayes, Walter: *The Captain from Nantucket and the Mutiny on the Bounty*, 1996.

Hollister G.H.: *The History of Connecticut*, Vol 2, 1855.

Howse, Derek & Hutchinson, Beresford: *The Clocks & Watches of Captain James Cook*, Antiquarian Horology, 1969.

Markham, Sir Clements: *The Voyages of Pedro Fernandez de Quiros, 1595 to 1606.*

Mowat, H.G.: *Captain Carteret and the Voyage of the Swallow*, 2011.

Nautical Magazine & Naval Chronicle 1840: Cambridge Library Collection.

Naval Chronicle, January – July 1804 Clarke, James S & McArthur, John (Editors).

Nordoff, C. & Hall, J.N.: *Pitcairn's Island*, 1934.

Pitcairn Islands Philatelic Bureau, New Zealand.

Poland, Peter: *The Travels of the Timekeepers*, Woollahra History and Heritage Society, 1991.

Rigby, Nigel, van der Merwe, Pieter & Williams, Glyn: *Pioneers of the Pacific*, 2005.

Ronald D.A.B.: *Young Nelsons – Boy sailors during the Napoleonic Wars*, 2009.

Schecter, Barnet: *The Battle for New York*, 2002.

Shuldham, Molyneux: *The Despatches of Molyneux Shuldham* 1776, Edited by RW Neeser.

Sobel, Dava: *Longitude*, 1996.

Southey, Robert: *The Life of Nelson*, 1813.

Stackpole, Edouard A: *The Sea Hunters – The New England Whalemen During Two Centuries 1635-1835*, 1953.

Thompson, Edward: *The Meretriciad*, 1765.

van de Merwe, Pieter (Ed): *Nelson, An Illustrated History*, 2005.

Other Sources:

Admiral Digby Museum, Digby, Canada
Caird Library, National Maritime Museum, Greenwich, UK
Munroe Tavern Museum House, Lexington, New England, USA
Nantucket Historical Association, Nantucket, Massachusetts, USA
National Archives, Kew, Surrey, UK
National Portrait Gallery, London, UK
Royal Observatory, Royal Museums Greenwich, UK
Woollahra History and Heritage Society, Woollahra Municipal Library, Australia

Image Credits

Chapter	Part One

1   Pitcairn Island, "Rendered Impossible to Land"
NOAA National Oceanic and Atmospheric Photo
Library / The Dolphin and The Swallow, from
Carteret: 'Voyage Round the World 1766-1769' /
Discovering Pitcairn 1767 Commemorative Stamp,
courtesy of Pitcairn Islands Philatelic Bureau.

2   The Wreck of The Association, unknown artist c
1710, National Maritime Museum, Greenwich,
London (PAH0710, image 1034).

3   Larcum Kendall K1 Timekeeper, 1769, National
Maritime Museum, Greenwich, London ZAA0038
(L7650-001) / Larcum Kendall K2 Timekeeper,
1771, National Maritime Museum, Greenwich,
London ZAA0078 (L5494-001) / Larcum Kendall
K3 Timekeeper, 1774, National Maritime Museum,
Greenwich, London ZAA0111 (L5475-001).

4   The Racehorse and The Carcass 1773, John
Cleveley, from Phipps: 'A Voyage Towards the
North Pole...' 1774 / Cancer Boreas from Phipps: 'A
Voyage towards the North Pole...' 1774.

5   Paul Revere's Ride, US National Archives (NAID
535721) / Major Pitcairn entering Lexington, from
James Grant: 'British Battles on Land and Sea' 1897
/ The Old Brown Bess of 1786 from James Grant:
'British Battles on Land and Sea' 1897 / 'Turtle'

Submarine, from William Oliver Stevens: ''A History of Seapower', 1920.

6   Prince William Henry serving as midshipman on HMS Prince George – Benjamin West, 1782, National Maritime Museum, Greenwich, London (PAH5531).

9   Bligh cartoon – reproduced by kind permission of Ken Pyne / Private Eye Magazine.

10   HMS Pandora founders on the Barrier Reef 1779, etching by Robert Batty, from Sir John Barrow: 'The Eventful History of the Mutiny...' 1831

First Image Section After Chapter 10

Royal Observatory, Greenwich c 1770, National Maritime Museum, Greenwich, London (L7159 - AST0042) / Pitcairn Island, NASA image by Lawrence Ong & EO-1 team / Sir Cloudesley Shovell – c 1702-05, Michael Dahl, National Maritime Museum, Greenwich, London (BHC3025) / Larcum Kendall K2 Timekeeper, 1771, National Maritime Museum, Greenwich, London (L5494-001) / Nelson and the Bear: Richard Westall 1806, National Maritime Museum, Greenwich, London (BHC2907) / Pitcairn Pistols, courtesy Doug Mindell and Lexington Historical Society / The Asia in Halifax Harbour c 1797, George Gustavus Lennock, Library and Archives, Canada, (R9266-307), Peter Winkworth Collection of Canadiana / Admiral Robert Digby, Courtesy Admiral Digby Museum, Nova Scotia, Canada / The Coming of the Loyalists 1783, Henry Sandham 1842-1910, Library and Archives,

Canada (1996-282-7) / Chart of the Western Coast of Africa, engraved by Thomas Kitchin c 1770, (author's collection) / Portrait of Rear Admiral William Bligh, Alexander Huey, 1814, National Library of Australia nla.obj-1948360 / Matavai Bay, Tahiti, William Hodges c 1776, Yale Center for British Art, Paul Mellon Collection (B1981.25-343) / The Bounty – replica entering Ostend harbour, by Yasmina, 2009 (cc by 3.0) / Bligh Leaving The Bounty, Robert Dodd, c 1790, National Maritime Museum, Greenwich, London (PY9205).

Part Two

11 An Island in Time, J Folger, courtesy Nantucket Historical Association / Moby Dick, Augustus Burnham Shute, illustration from book by Herman Melville, 1892 edition / Queequeg, I W Taber, illustration from book 'Moby Dick' by Herman Melville, 1902 edition / The ice islands, seen the 9th of Janry., 1773. Engrav'd by B T Pouncy; drawn from nature by W Hodges. London, 1777. Alexander Turnbull Library, National Library of New Zealand, Wellington, New Zealand. (C-051-016).

12 A Fur Seal, C Landseer, 1848, from Henry W Elliot monograph-Seal Islands 1873.

13 Mayhew Folger c 1810, photograph from the original, courtesy of the Massillon Museum OH, USA / John Adams, from 'Voyages aux Iles du Grand Ocean' by Jacques.Antoine Moerenhout, 1837 p284 / John Adams' House, built by himself, from T B Murray: 'The home of the mutineers' 1854

/ 'Everyday Fletcher Christian thought of Greenwich', by C Ashcroft, (author's collection).

16 Sir Thomas Herbert, J H Lynch c 1850, National Maritime Museum, Greenwich, London (PW3591) / Attack on First Bar Battery, Canton River, from Edward Belcher: 'Narrative of a Voyage Round the World' Vol II 1843 / Chinese sketch of an English Sailor, from J A Green: 'A Short History of the English People' 1894 / HMS Blenheim c 1825, from James Orange 'The Chater Collection: Pictures relating to China, Hong Kong, Macao' 1924.

17 Royal Observatory, Greenwich 2007 by M R Dryland.

Second Image Section After Chapter 10

Captain Folger on Pitcairn, Courtesy of the Pitcairn Islands Philatelic Bureau / The Pitcairn Porcelain given to Captain Folger with K2, courtesy of the Nantucket Historical Association / First Opium War Conflict Overview Map, by Philg88, (cc by 4.0) / Map of the Island of Nantucket, Dr James Tupper 1772, Courtesy of the Nantucket Historical Association / Destroying Chinese War Junks 1841, Edward Duncan 1843, National Maritime Museum, Greenwich, London (PY8192).

Epilogues

Captain Peter Heywood, John Simpson 1822, National Maritime Museum, Greenwich, London (BHC2766) / Countenance of a Female Fur Seal, Henry W Elliot monograph-Seal Islands 1873 / Fleecing the Carcass of a Fur Seal, Henry W Elliot monograph-Seal Islands 1873 / Northern Elephant Seal, Henry W Elliot monograph-Seal Islands 1873.

John Bendall. A background in economic history, political science and marketing and is now an independent researcher living in Greenwich. John has a long-standing love of the Royal Observatory and National Maritime Museum, Greenwich, including the Caird Library. He is a member of the Society for Nautical Research and Nantucket Historical Association, which have both provided interesting material, as has the National Archives in West London. This book was inspired by American author Dava Sobel's renowned 'Longitude', covering Harrison's timepieces in revolutionising maritime navigation. John has researched a fascinating follow-up story of Larcum Kendall and the K2 timekeeper. John is also a director of an English language school in Canterbury and a document management services company. His supportive wife, Jane, worked at the NMM for many years and is founder of the Flamsteed Astronomy Society.

Mike Dryland. Mike retired from a career in industry in 2001 and has since been spending time as a voluntary curatorial assistant at the Royal Observatory, Greenwich, where he specialises in tours and talks about the Harrison marine timekeepers (sea clocks) and the history of the Observatory. He studied physics and has a long-time interest in astronomy, horology and naval history. Mike contributed two chapters and the appendix for this book, and helped generally with navigation and horology issues.

Acknowledgements

My first thanks must be to my wife, Jane; and family, including Nick, Catherine, Natalie and their fine spouses, who have all been supportive.

I am indebted to long-standing friend Mike Dryland for his technical input, his vision and as valued co-author for the more technical sections. I am grateful to Rory McEvoy, who was Curator of Horology at the Royal Observatory, Greenwich, for his perception and expertise in writing the Foreword for this book.

Pieter van der Merwe, MBE, is a highly experienced and well-known maritime specialist who has been generous with his time and advice.

My thanks to Silvia Crompton for her initial editing and also to Steve Bagnold for his advice. Further thanks to Norman, Tim, John, James, Mike, Pam and other pals for unfailing goodwill. My grandson James, and daughter, Catherine Ashcroft have been very helpful on the technical front.

A big thanks to the unsung heroes and heroines working at historical information centres, including the Caird Library at the Greenwich National Maritime Museum, The National Archives, The Society of Nautical Research, The National Portrait Gallery, Woollahra History and Heritage Society in Australia, Munroe Tavern Museum House in Lexington, Admiral Digby Museum in Canada, Pitcairn Island Philatelic Bureau in New Zealand, and The Nantucket Historical Association.

Finally, my thanks to Austin Macauley Publishers Ltd.